Windows 7 Utility programs

Estimated time: **3 hours**

After completion of this module you will be able to use the following :

- Calculator
- Paint
- Wordpad
- Notepad
- Windows fax and scan
- Windows live moviemaker
- Media player(playing music)
- Windows photo gallery
- Windows live mail
- Windows Live Messenger
- PDF reader
- XPS reader
- MSN Messenger

Utility programs(With windows 7 the following programs are also available):

Notepad, wordpad, calculator,paint,windows live photo gallery,windows live mail,windows fax and scan

Notepad

Notepad is a program where you can add words and save the words to a file.

The white spaced area is where you type your letter in notepad.

Press the spacebar,(the long rectangular bar) to create a space between 2 words

Press enter to create a new line in notepad

Saving the file

➢ Click on <File> and on <save> to save the document to the disk drive.

Practise exercise : Notepad

Type in the information below and save the file

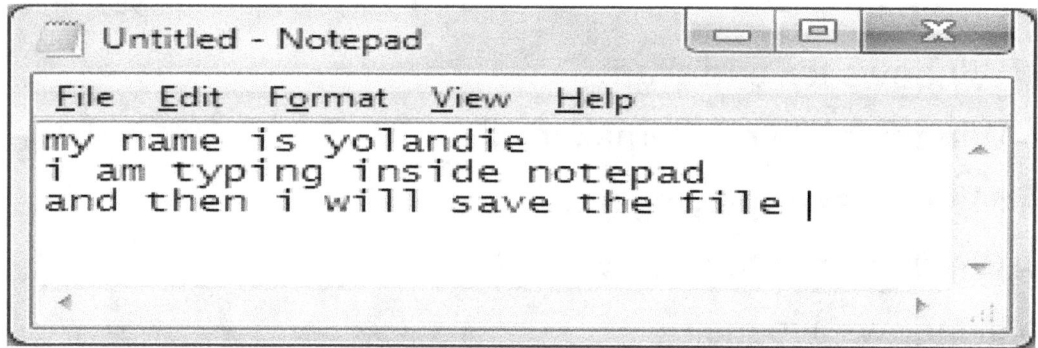

Wordpad

Wordpad is a program where you can add words and save it to disk. WordPad allows you to do basic formatting, however it does not have all the features that Microsoft word has. The functions in wordpad works the same as in notepad, however WordPad have more functions.

Practise exercise: Wordpad

Type in the following data, and save the file

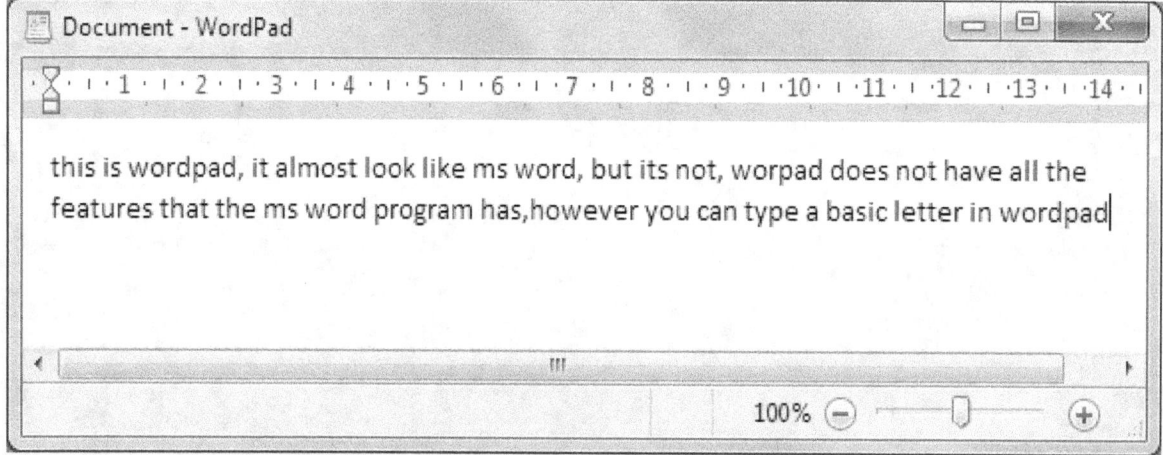

Printing a document

Print preview

Print preview is an option that allows you to view on screen, what the document will look like before it is printed out on paper.

> ➢ Click on, ▦ move the cursor over the print option and click on print preview

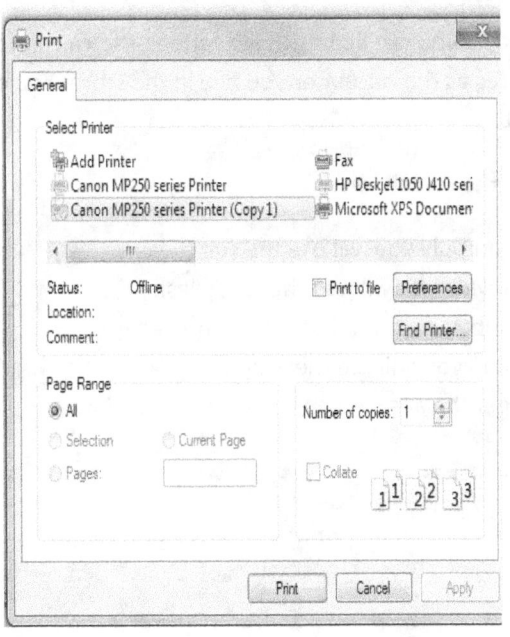

Print options

Click on ▦, Print

Choose printer driver

> ✦ Select a printer, click on the printer driver that has the same name as your printer

Page Range:

> ✦ Selecting all, will print all the pages
> ✦ Clicking on selection will print only the part that has been selected in the document
> ✦ Current page, will print only the page where the mouse cursor is currently at
> ✦ Pages : typing in<1,8> will print only pages 1 and 8
> ✦ Pages: typing in <1-8 >will print from page 1 up to page 8

Copies

> ✦ If you want to print more than one copy of the same document, just type in the number of copies that you want, or click on the up or down arrow to increase or decrease the number of copies.

Collate

Select the Collate option to print all the pages in order before printing extra copies.

If you chose to make 2 copies of 4 pages, activating collate will print the following order, pages:1234,1234.

Uncollated will print in the following order: 11,22,33,44

Preferences

Page orientation

> ➢ Click on preferences, page orientation: click on the up or down arrow to change to landscape or portrait option

Page quality

> ➢ Click on preferences, click at the top on the <paper quality tab> Choose best, using more ink, printing a darker quality, or choose <draft> using less ink

Print queue management

After you have selected, the print option, the document is now send to the printer. If you now want to cancel the print request you will have to use the print queue management function.

> ➢ Click on start, devices and printers
> ➢ Click on the active printer, right click
> ➢ Select <see what's printing>
>   *A list of documents that have been send to the printer will be available.*
> ➢ Click on <document> on the menu and click on <cancel> if you don't want to print the document, click on pause if you want the printing to stop only temporarily.

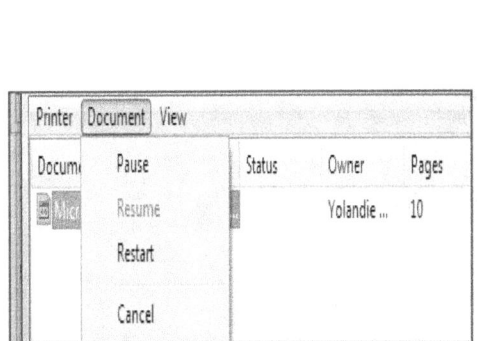

Calculator

With calculator you can do basic calculations The calculator that's included in windows 7 has the same features as the calculator you buy in the store. You can add, subtract, divide and multiply with the calculator.

How to use the calculator:

➢ To multiply you will use the star *
➢ To divide you will use the backslash /
➢ To subtract you will use the minus – sign
➢ To add you will use the + sign
➢ To get the answer you will use the equal = sign.

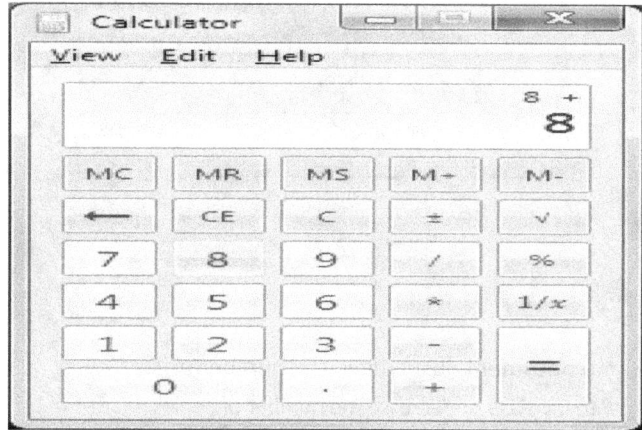

Practise exercise: Calculator: 10 +2 = 12

➢ Move the arrow key to the number 1 and left click once
➢ Move the arrow key to the number 0 and left click once
➢ Move the arrow key to + plus sign and left click once
➢ Move the arrow key to the number 2 and left click once
➢ Move the cursor to the equal sign and press ENTER (or press the left button once)
➢ Press C to clear

Practise exercise division 7divided by 7= 1

*Moving the cursor to an option and pressing left click once, means "**select**"*

7/7= 1

➢ Select 7
➢ Select /
➢ Select 7
➢ Select =

Paint

Paint is a program where you can do basic painting.

You can add different shapes that you can resize and format different colours

How to draw a basic shape in paint

You can use one of the autoshapes that have already been designed.

➢ Click on shape
➢ Select the shape you want
➢ Position the arrow key to the starting position of the new drawing inside the white spaced area which is the drawing area
➢ Press down the left mouse button
➢ Move the cursor to the right and down to draw the shape bigger.
➢ Release the left mouse button when you are satisfied with the size of the shape.

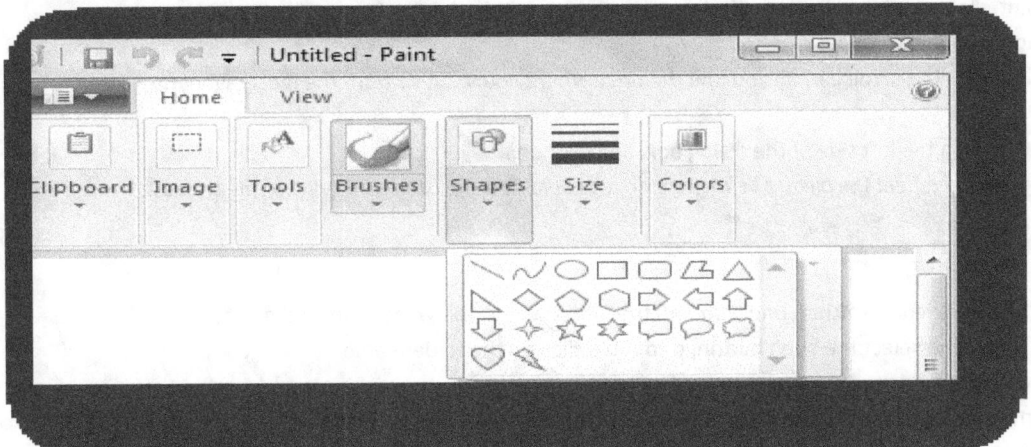

How to use the brush

You can also draw your own shapes with the brush

➢ Click on the brush to select any type of brush you want to use
➢ Click inside the drawing area, hold down the left button and drag the cursor to draw the line or shape that you wish to draw

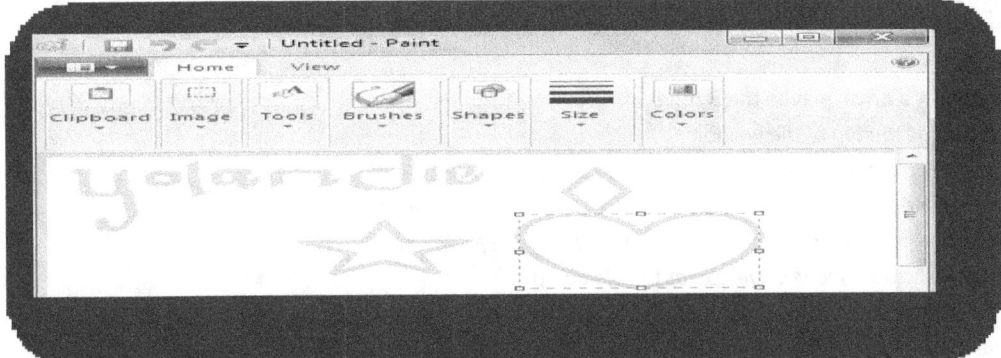

Saving a file

Click on 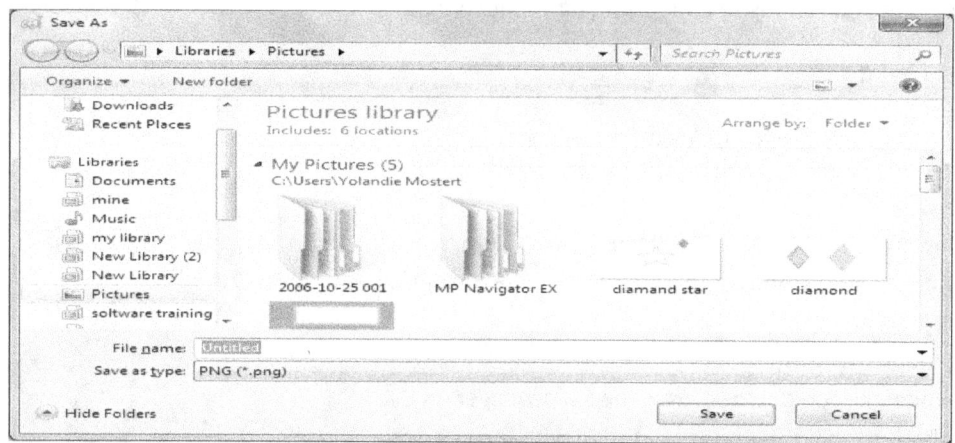 and on <save> or *Click on File and on <save>*

If you are saving a paint, file windows will automatically save it for you within the <pictures> <library>
However you may choose your own folder:

➢ Scroll down with the left scroll bar, till you find the drive where you want to store the file, maybe the D Drive,
➢ Locate the d drive on the left side of the dialog box, and click on it

The top of the window should reflect the picture below, the drive should now be listed at the top of the window.

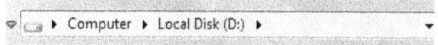

➢ Scroll down with the right scroll bar, until you find the folder where you want to store the data
➢ Click on the folder and select the open button, or double click on the folder name
   The folder name should now appear next to the local disk.
➢ Click inside the white rectangular box next to the word filename, that says untitled and
➢ Type in a descriptive filename of your choice
   The filename <untitled> will be overwritten by the new name that you typed in.

➢
➢ Notice that paint will automatically give it an extension name png,
   Wordpad has an extension ,rtf and notepads extension is txt

Creating a new folder inside a program
If you forgot to create a folder in the windows explorer to save your data in, you can create a folder while you are saving your file:

➢ Click on file save, select a drive, maybe the D drive.
➢ Click on <new folder> *at the top of the window*
   A <newfolder >name is created and is listed in the dialog box on the right side
➢ Type in a descriptive folder name, this name will replace the folder name that was created
➢ Click on the new folder, and click on <open>, *or double click on the folder name*
   The new folder name should appear at the top of the dialog box
➢ Type in a descriptive filename and
➢ Click on the save button

Windows live photo gallery

Photo gallary is a tool, to manage your pictures. You can slightly adjust the background color of your pictures with some of the photo galery options. You can also resize your pictures and you can sort your pictures according to dates,rates,flags and tags. You can create a slide show of selected pictures and send certain pictures via photo galary to your friends Email.

Rating pictures

You can rate your picture, 1,2,3,4 and 5 star, and then sort them according to the stars. For example you can rate the best quality picture a 3 or 5 star, and a picture that doesn't have good quality you can rate a 1 or 2. With this function you can quickly find quality pictures.

How to rate a picture

> Left click on the picture and then
> click on the down arrow , next to rate, the rate option on the left side
> click on the rating option, for example 4 star or 2 star

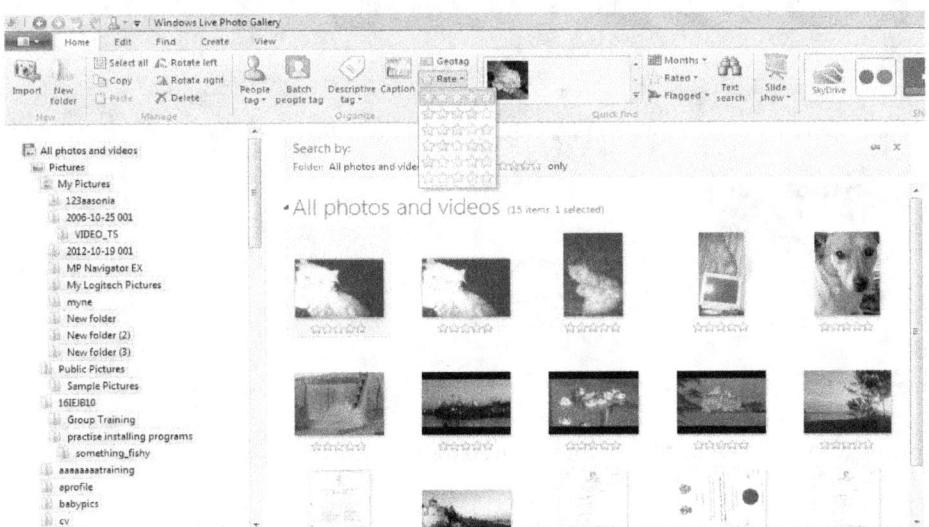

How to sort your pictures according to rate

> Left click on the down arrow next to the word rate on the right side of the screen
> Click on the rating of your choice, then only pictures of that rating will be visible

Adding flags to pictures

> ➢ Click on the picture and then left click once on the flag option on the left side

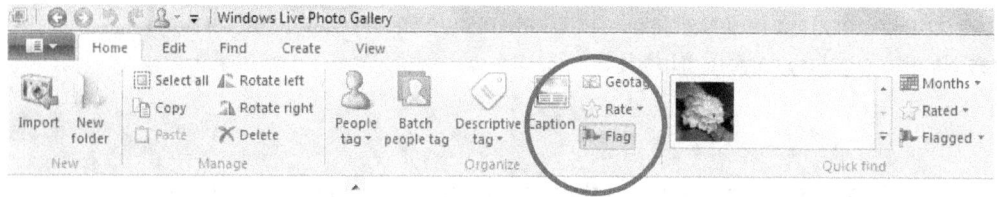

How to browse only flagged pictures

> ➢ Left click on the flagged option on the right side

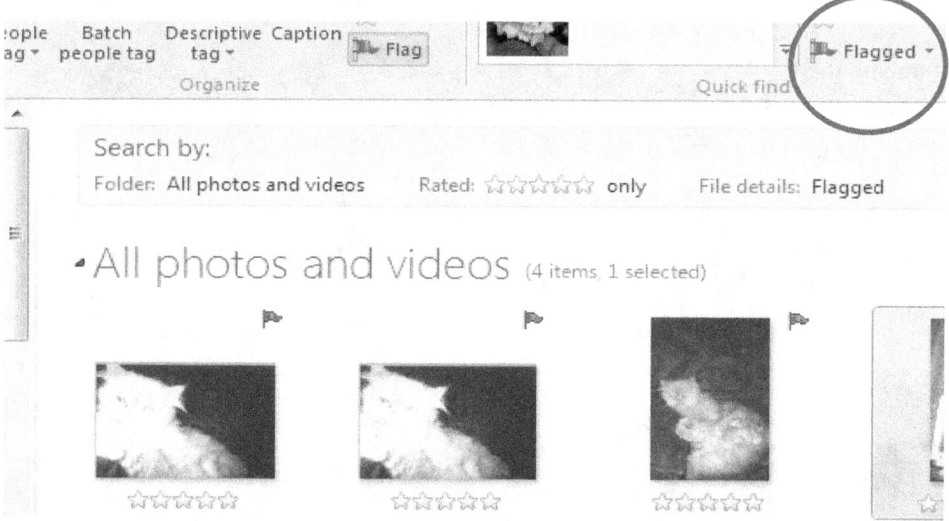

Viewing your pictures according to date

> ➢ Click on the down arrow next to month and click on the desired date

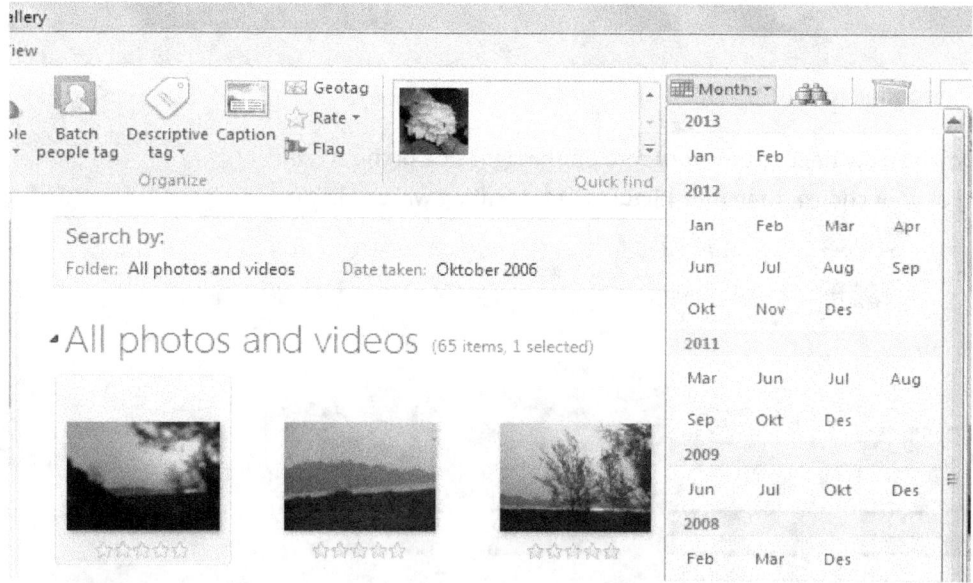

Changing the exposure

> ➢ Click on the down arrow underneath the word exposure
> ➢ Click on the option of your choice

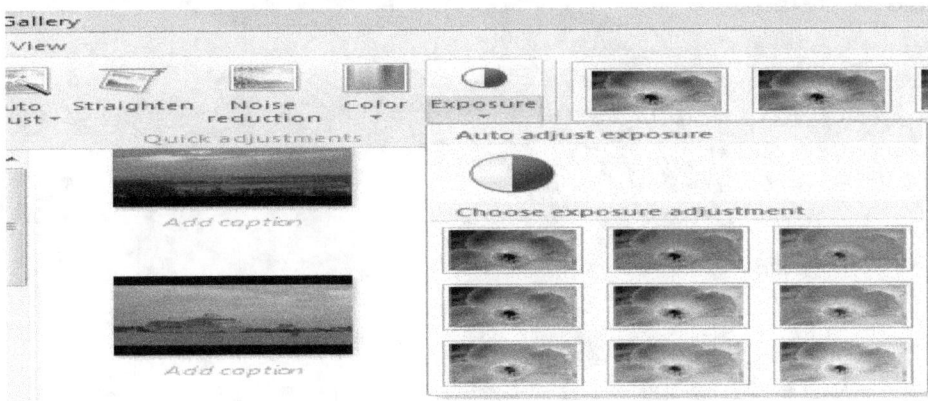

Enhancing the color in the picture

> ➢ Click on any of the <effects> of your choice.

Notice that these effect options add different colors into the background of your picture

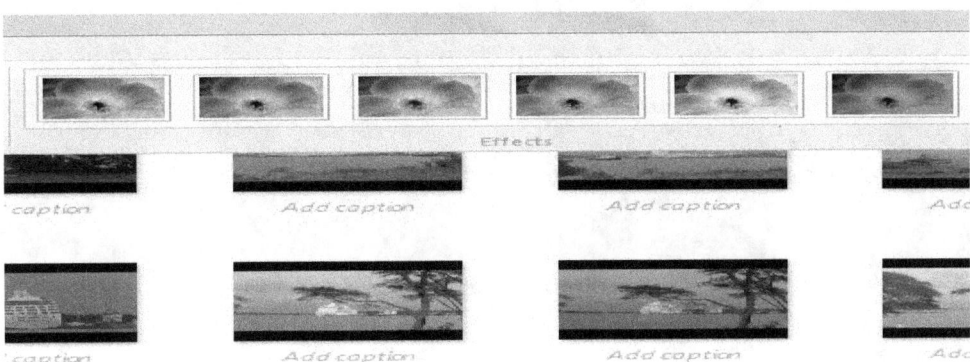

Choose color adjustment

> ➢ Click on the down arrow beneath color and
> ➢ Click on the option of your choice

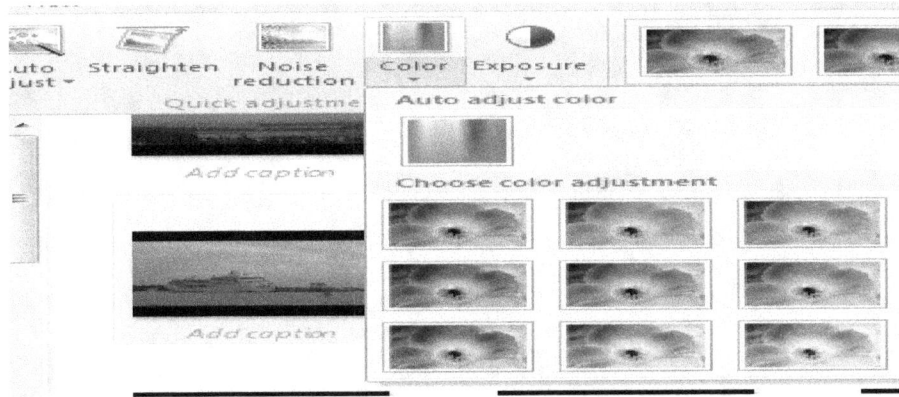

Sending pictures via Email using photogallery

- ➢ Click on create,photo Email
- ➢ Select either send photo email or attachment

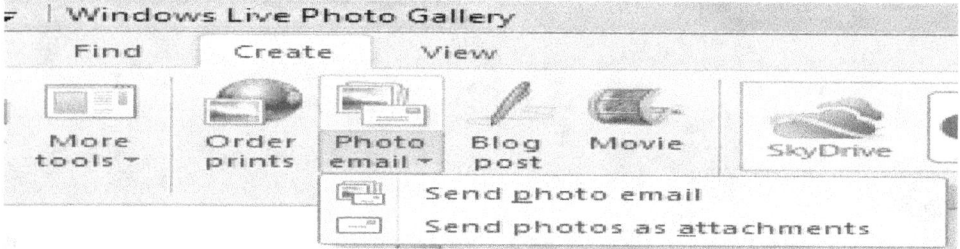

Send photo Email

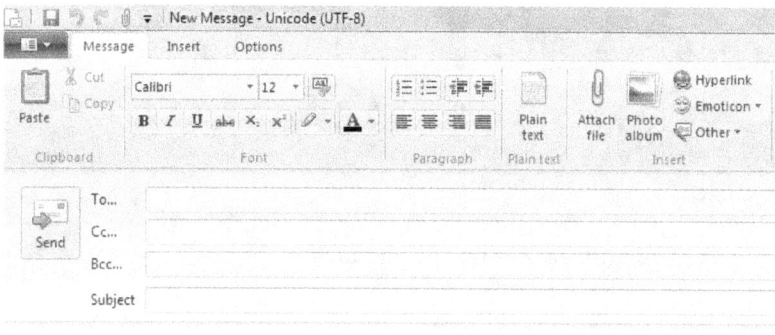

Enter album name here

VIEW SLIDE SHOW   DOWNLOAD ALL
This album has 1 photo and will be available on SkyDrive until 2013/05/05.

Send attachment

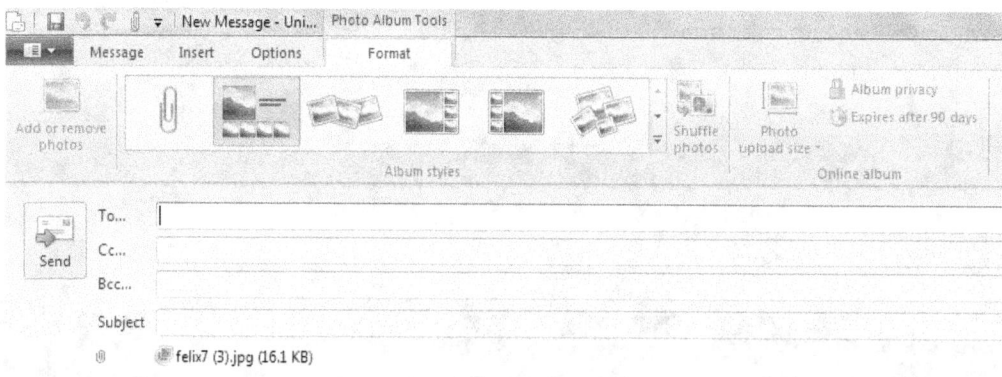

Creating a slideshow

A slide show is a selection of pictures that will be displayed full screen one by one after each other.

> ➢ Hold down the control key and click on all the folders you want to include in the slideshow
> ➢ Click on the down arrow next to slideshow
> ➢ Click on desired slideshow theme, the slide show will start showing each picture full screen.

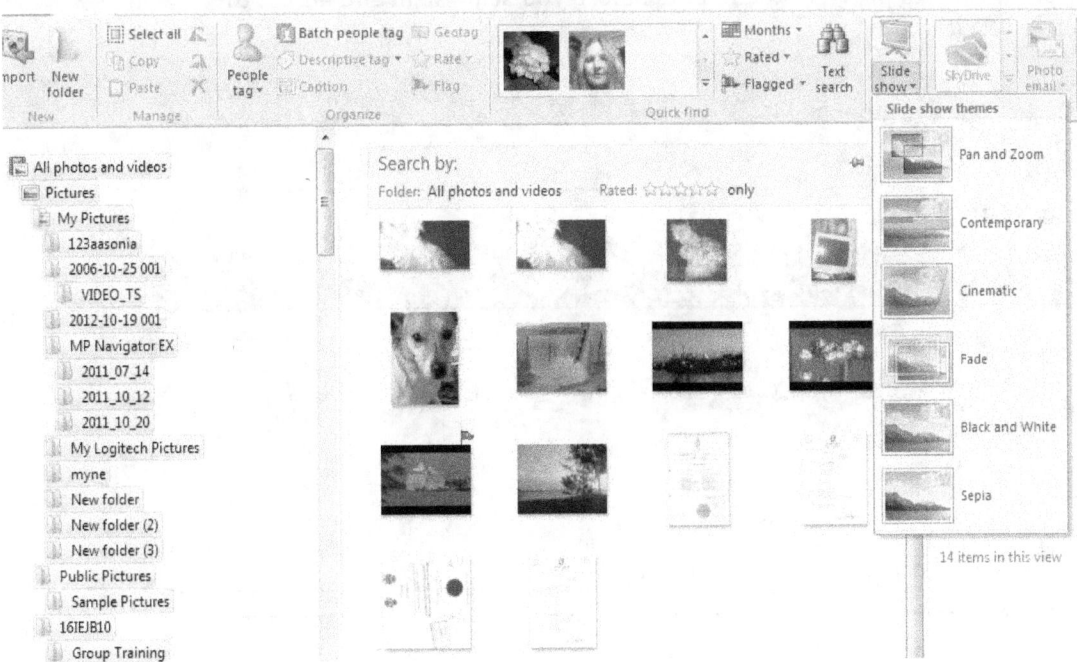

You can also create a movie from selected pictures

> ➢ Select pictures and then Click on create , Movie

Changing the size of a picture
You can adjust the size of the picture, many times we want a smaller file size on a webpage, yet however keep in mind that if the picture is too small, you will lose quality in the picture.

> ➢ Click on edit, resize

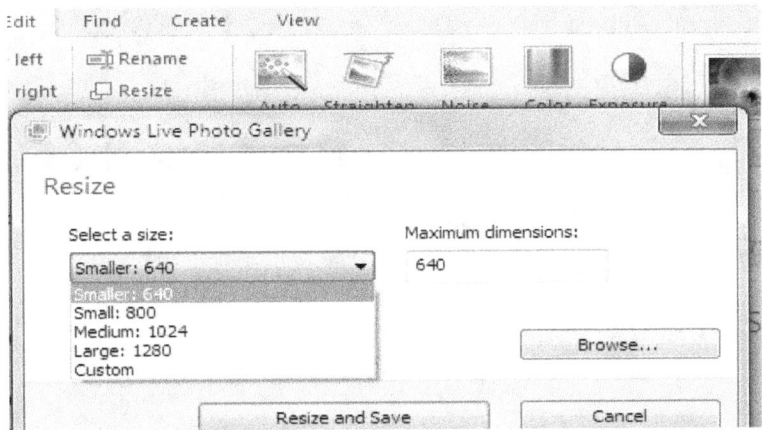

Windows fax and scan

With windows fax and scan you can receive and send faxes via your computer

You will need a fax modem to use windows fax and scan as a fax machine

To scan documents with windows fax and scan you need to connect a scanner

With windows scan, You can preview documents before you scan them and adjust the settings for better results

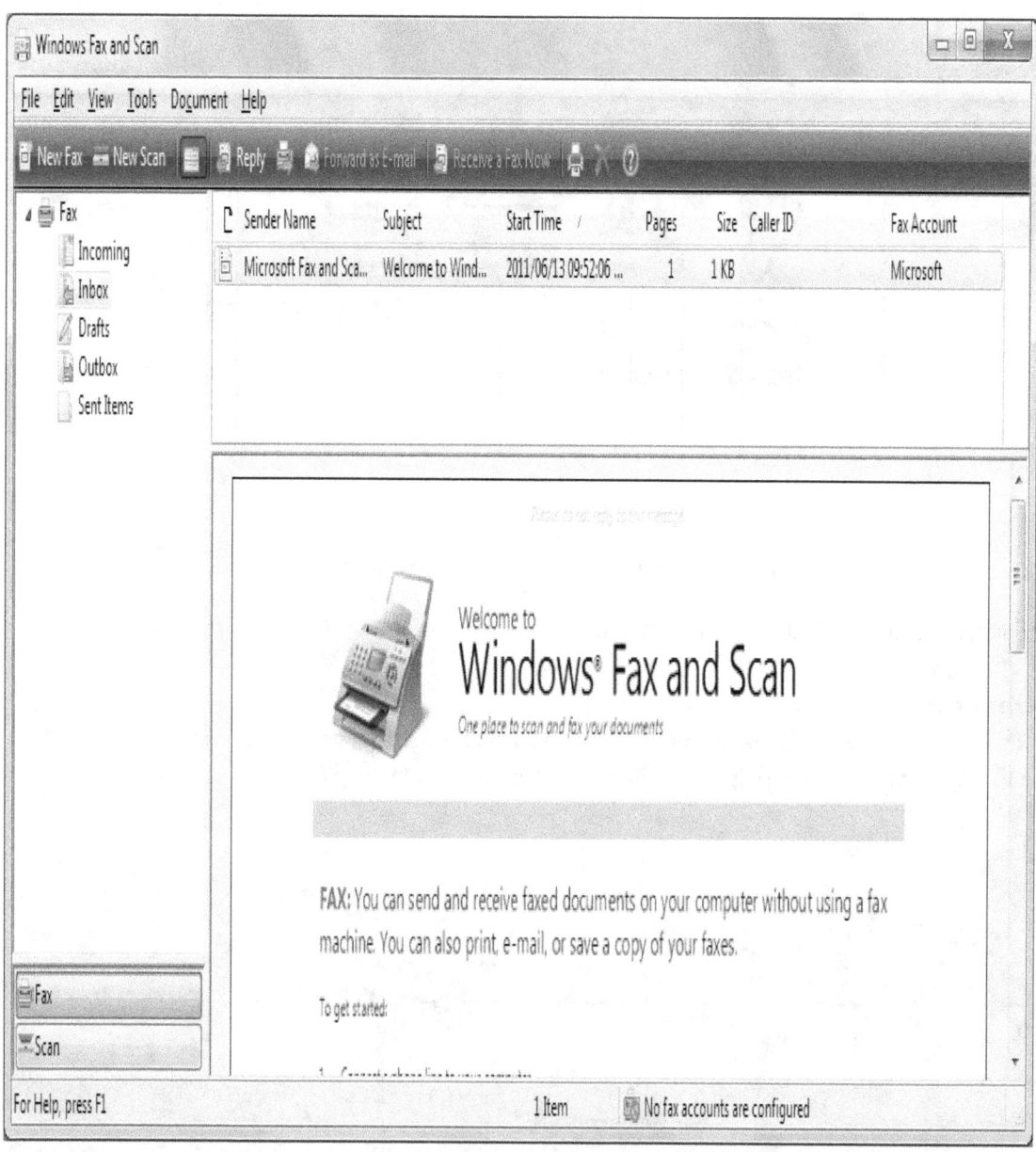

Windows live mail

Creating an Email

Forwarding mail

Replying to Email

Attaching documents

Schedule an event

Creating a message rule

With windows live mail, you can send and receive documents and schedule your tasks and keep a list of contact details.

➢ Click on <start> all programs <windows live> to start the program.

To schedule tasks you don't need to be connected to the internet, to receive email you must be connected to the internet

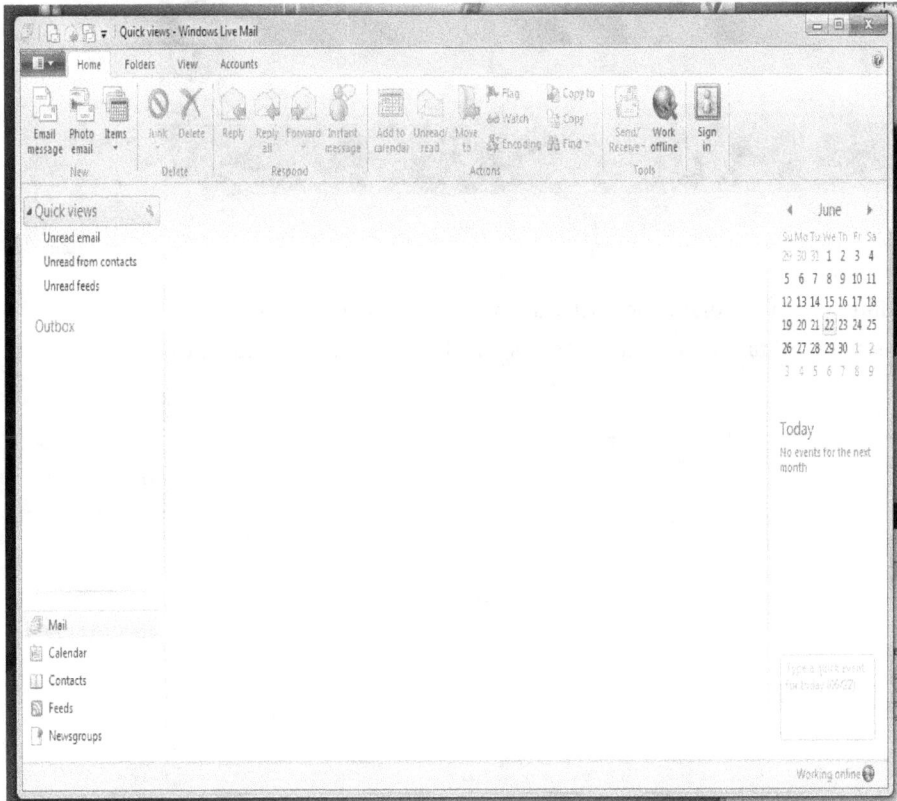

To schedule your tasks

> ➤ Click on calendar
> ➤ Double click on the date you want to schedule an event

After you typed in the information, make sure to click on the <Save and close> button to store the information into the program

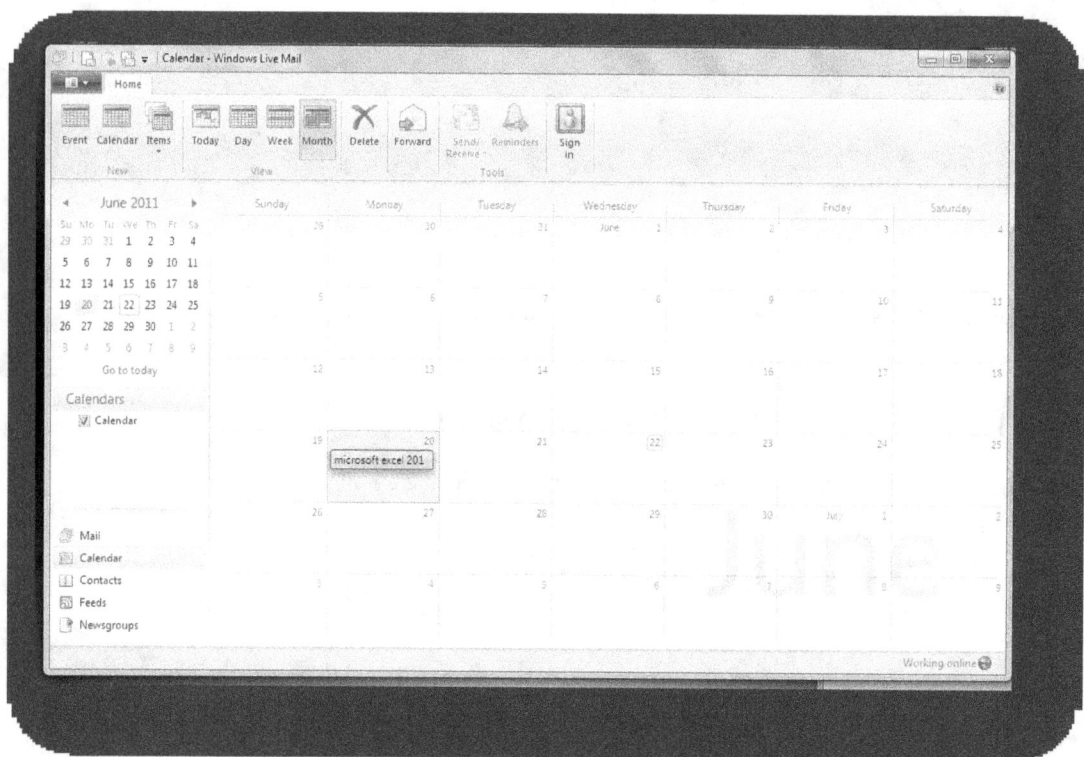

After you double clicked on the date, the event dialog box will appear, where you can type in detailed information about your scheduled task and decide if this is an all day event or schedule the hours.

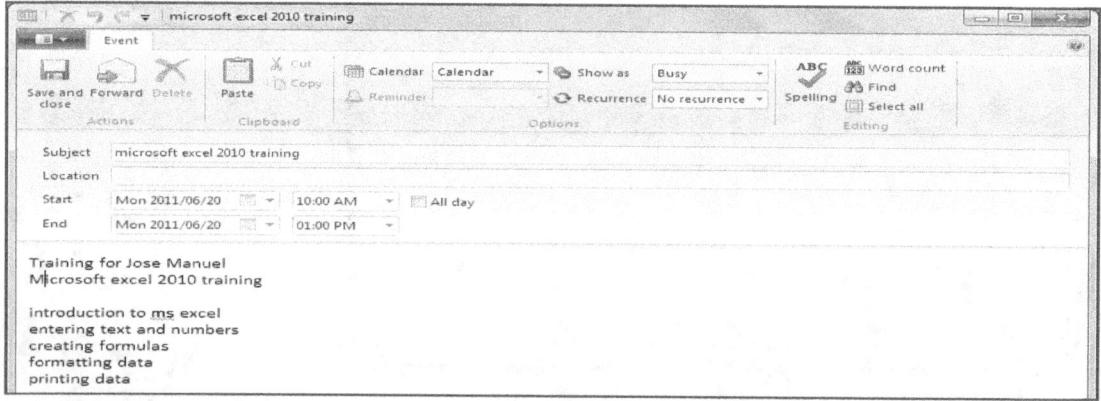

> ➤ Click on the up or down arrow to change the date and time or type in the time

Writing an Email message

How to create an email

On the left top corner click on email message, the email dialog box will appear

➢ Click inside the <to> option and write the email address of the person you are sending it to
➢ Click inside the <subject> option and tell the recipient what the letter content is
➢ Click underneath subject in the white square and start typing your letter
➢ Click on spell check after typing the letter to fix spelling mistakes
➢ Click on attachment if you have a file you want to send with this letter
➢ Click on formatting options to enhance your letters appearance

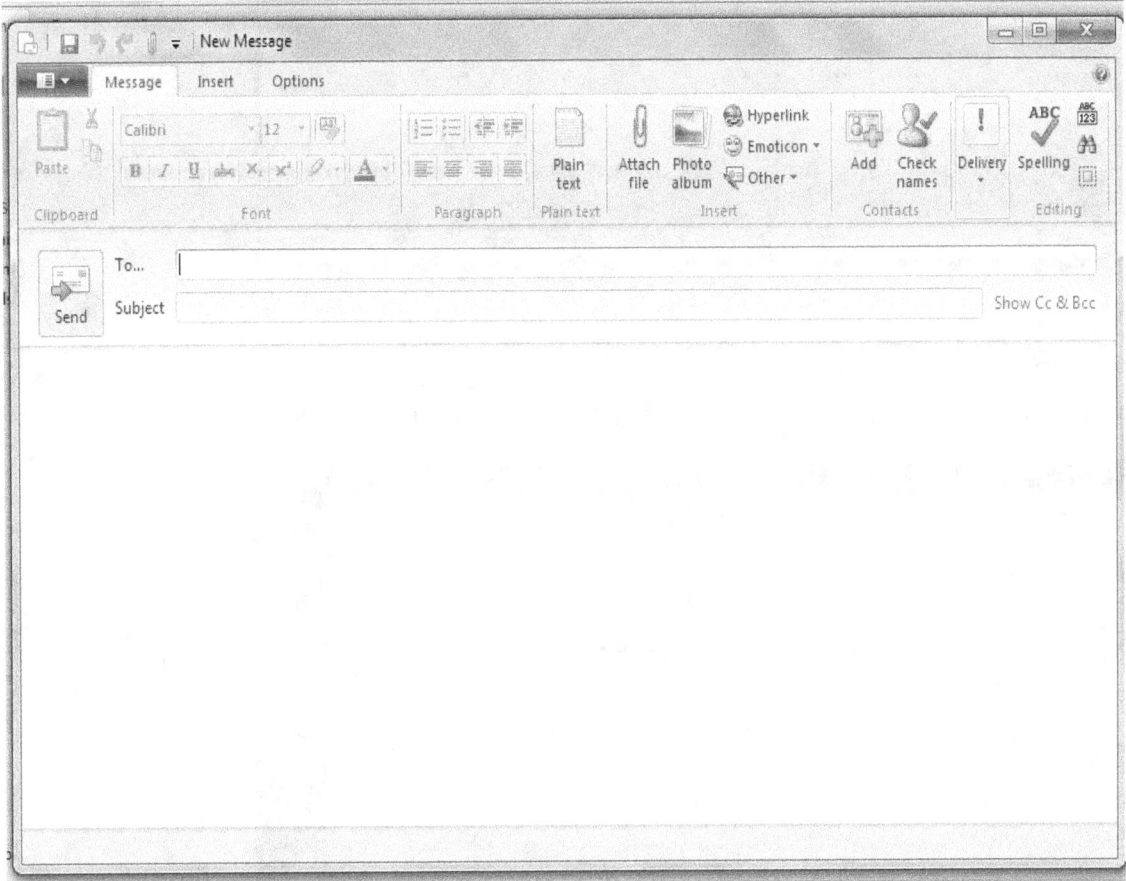

Replying to messages

Replying to a message means that after you have read the email you will be writing a response and sending it to the same person

Forwarding messages

You can forward a message you received from one person to another person by using the forward option

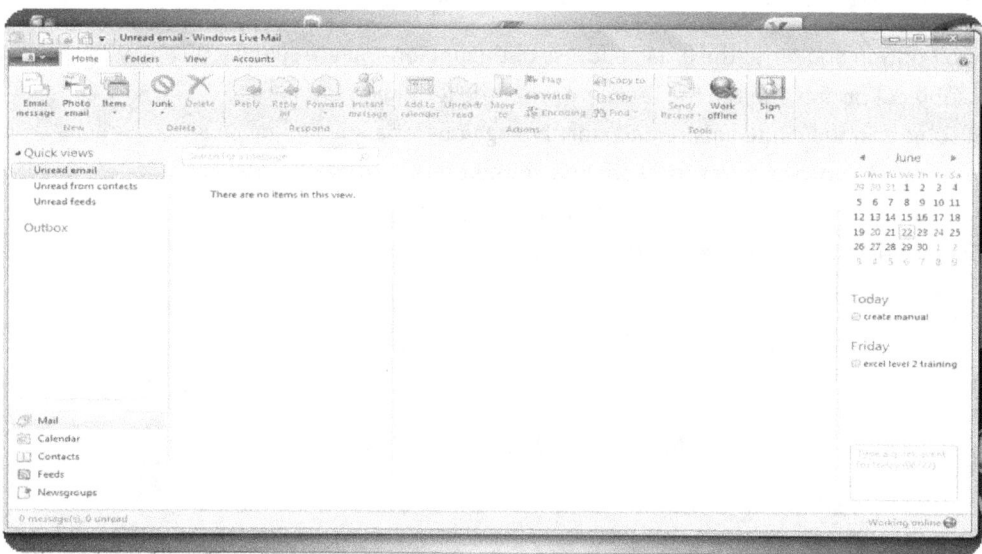

Message rule

With windows live you can manage your received messages with the message rule function

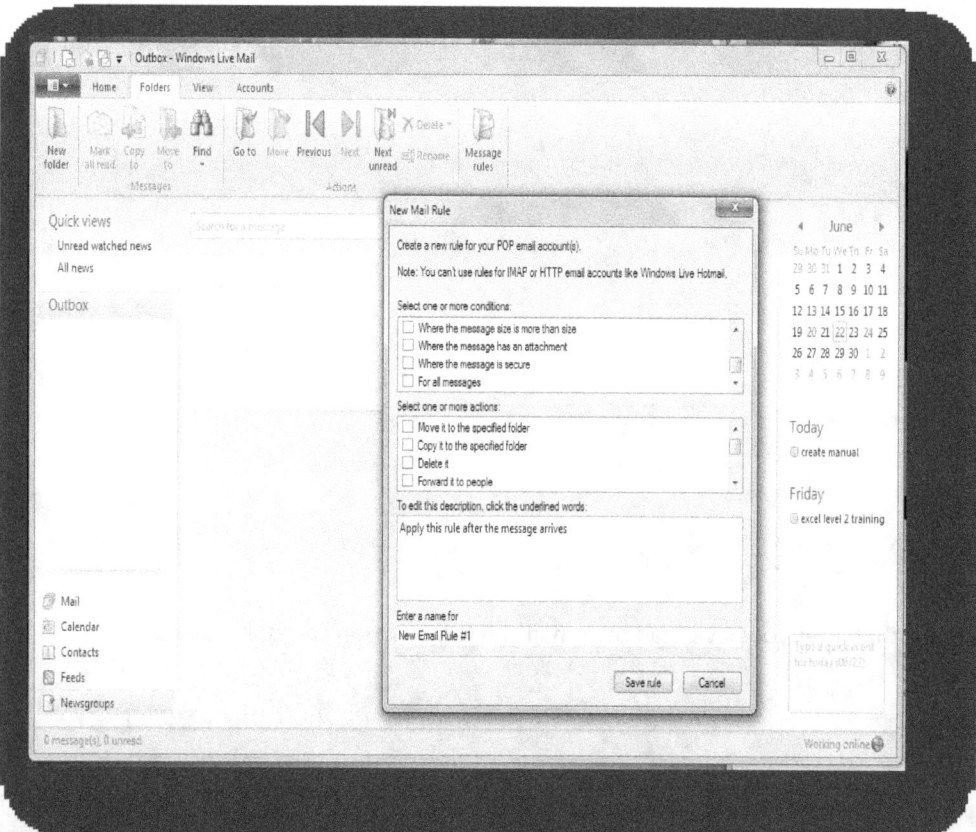

Windows media player

With windows media player you can play music and copy music and translate music to a different format

When inserting a disk into the cd drive windows media player will start playing the cd.

To go to Windows Media player library click on the right upper corner to go to the library.

You can copy(rip) music to your library and create your own playlist

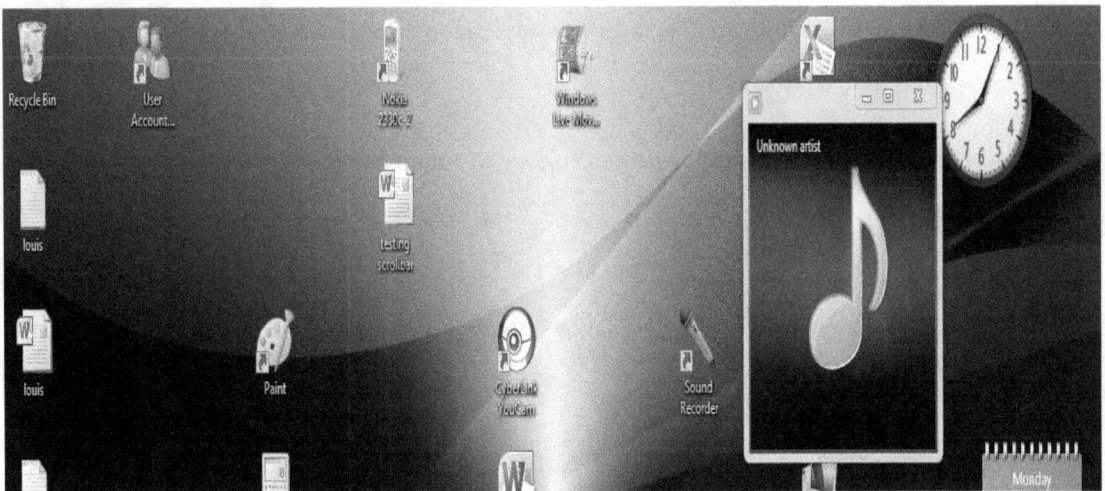

Creating your own playlist

> click on create playlist to create your own play list

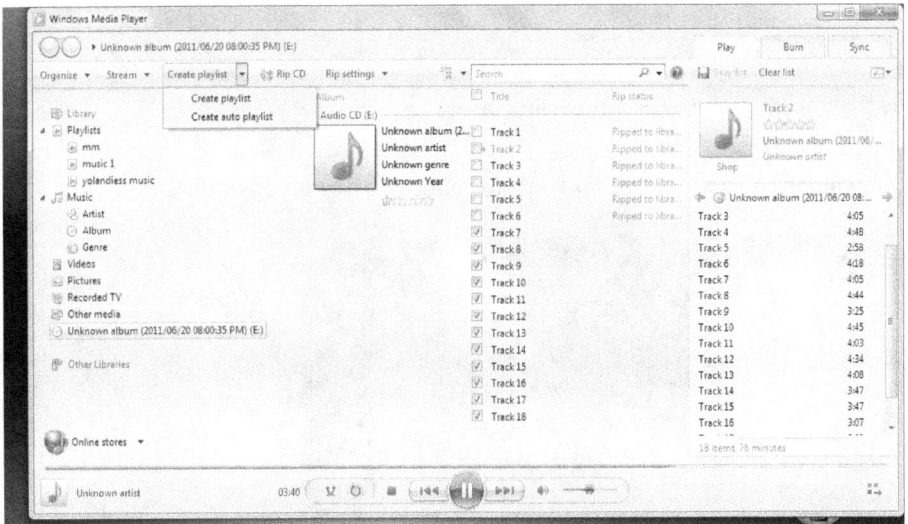

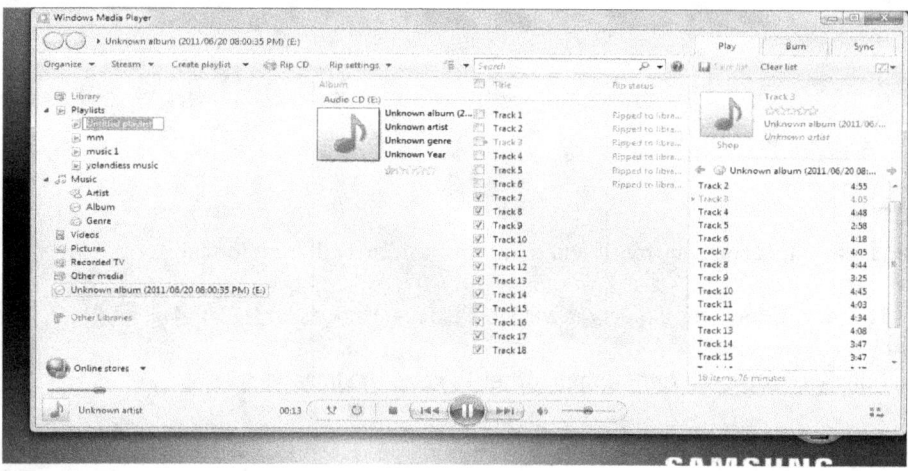

Copying music from your CD to your windows media player library is called ripping.

RIP CD

Once you have inserted a cd in the disk drive windows media player will open and the RIP to CD option will be available.

Copying music from your PC via windows media player is called burning

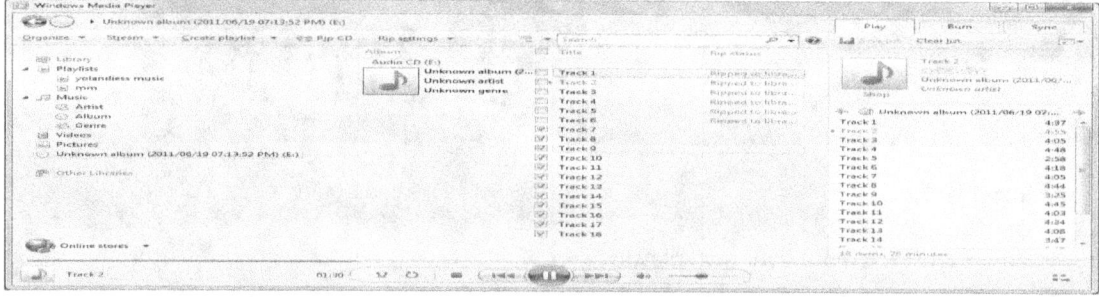

Burn CD

> Insert a new disk to copy the information to disk and select burn
> Drag the items you wish to burn to disk
> Click on start burning, this will take a few minutes for the information to be moved to disk.

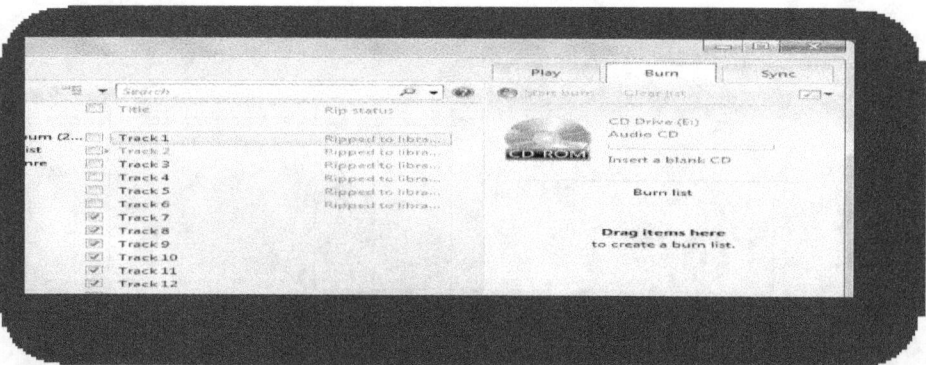

# Windows live Movie maker

With windows movie maker you can add sound and picture and record a video and add effects to your movie to make it more interesting

Starting  Windows Live Movie Maker

> ➢ Left Click on the start button, on the left bottom corner, and
> ➢ Left click once on windows live movie maker

If the program is not on your menu, click at the search option and type in <windows live movie maker>

windows live movie maker	×	Shut down ▸

Recording the movie

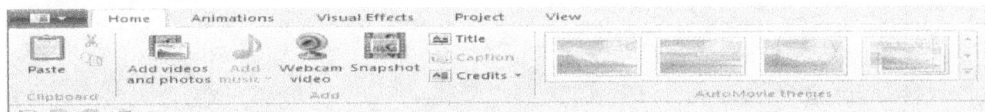

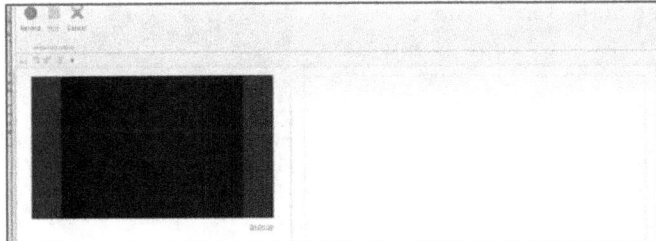

> ➢ Click on webcam video
> + When you are ready to start your movie recording, click on the red dot, that is the recorder button
> + When you have finished recording the video click on the blue square, which is the stop button
> + If you don't want to continue with the recording click on the red x, which is the cancel button

Saving the file

You will be prompted to give your video a filename

Provide a descriptive filename

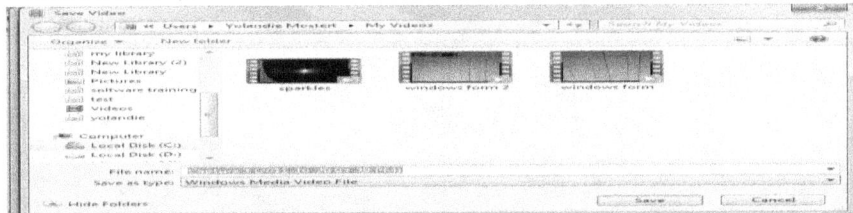

Adding a Title

Click on Title at the top of the menu on the left middle to add a title to your movie

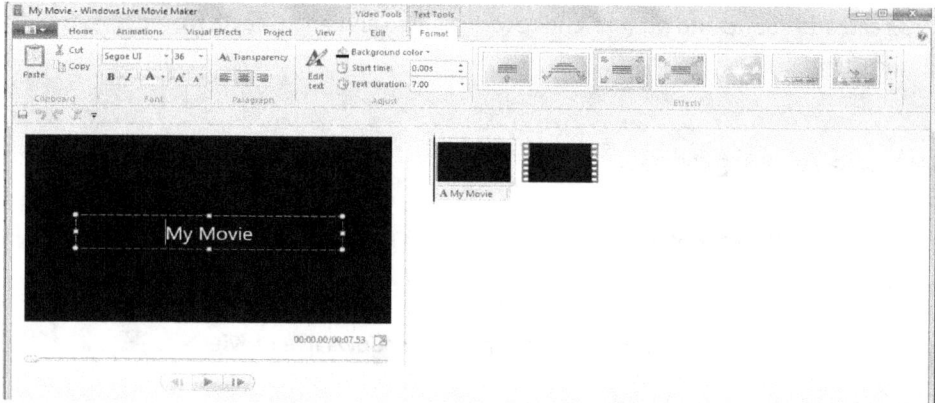

Type in the title of your move, example above is called <my movie>

Effects

On the right side of the screen there are effects that you can apply, to enhance the entrance of the title on the screen.

Left click on any of the effects to apply it to your screen.

The example below, are the cinema burst effect located at the top left menu

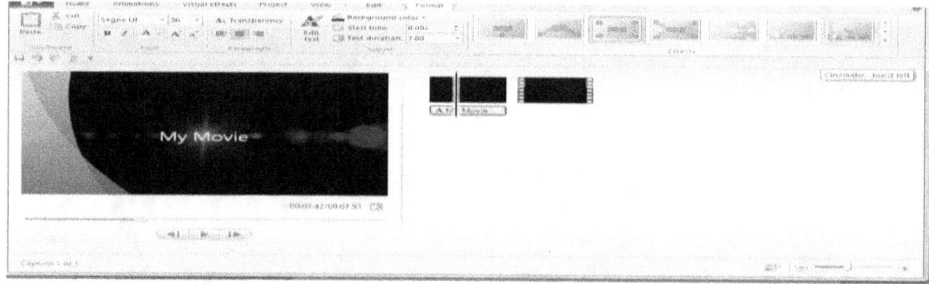

Click on the right arrow beneath the title, (the middle one) to play the movie

Caption

Click on caption to add words In a certain area in the movie

Play the movie and click on caption once you see the picture you want to add words to

Click on word effects at the top right of the screen to enhance the entrance of the words

The letters can fly in from the left or right or spin, choose the option you like

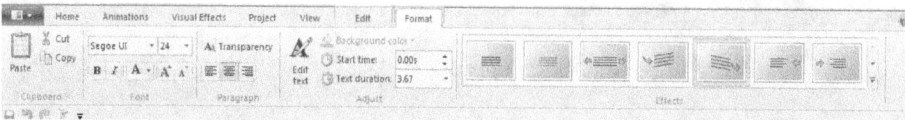

Credits

The names for the credits could be people that helped with the movie

- ➢ Click on the home tab and click on credits
- ➢ Type in the name that will appear at the end of the movie

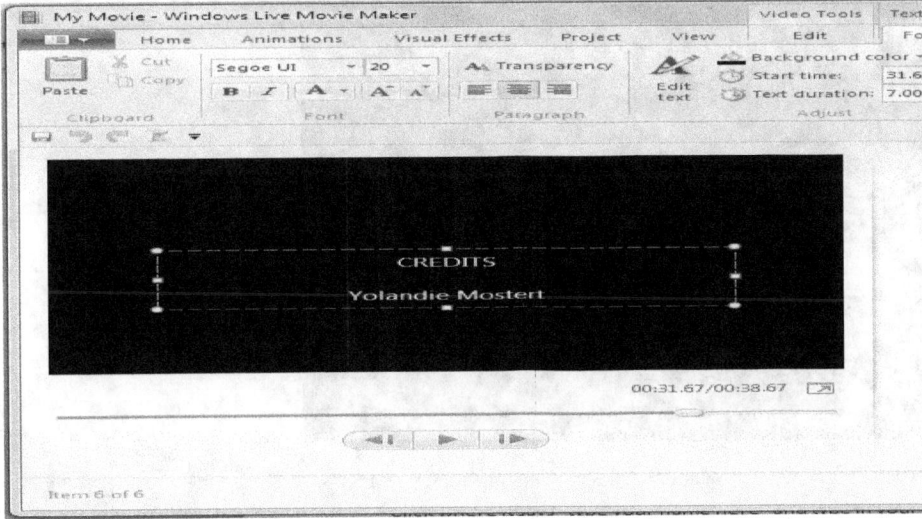

Directed by

The directed by is usually the name of the person that were directing the movie, the person in charge

- ➢ Click on the home tab, click on the down arrow next to credit and click on directed by
- ➢ Type in the name of the person who directed the movie, maybe you?

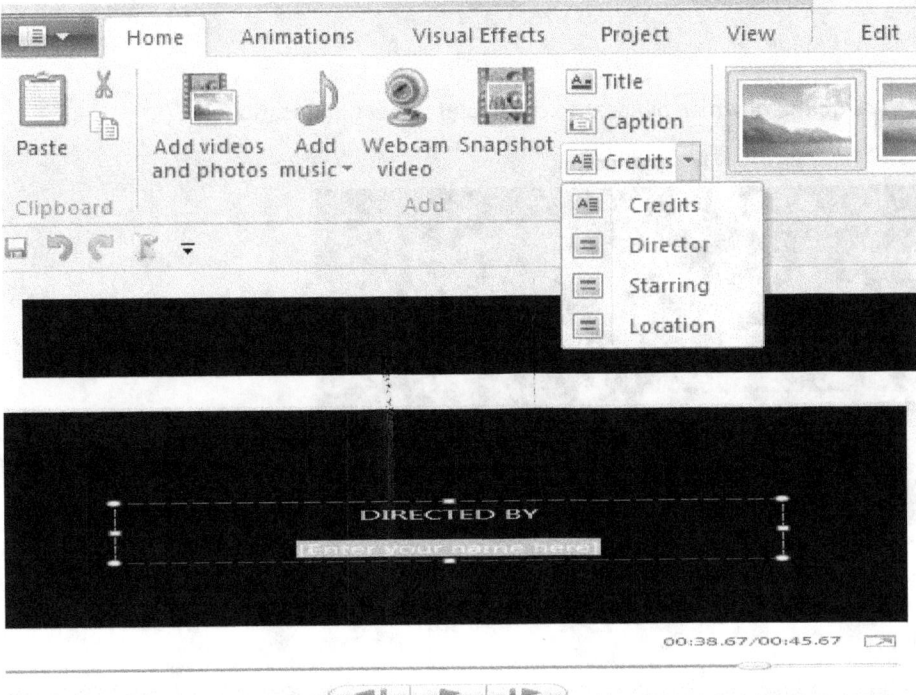

Starring

Starring is all the actors that played in the movie

➢ Click on home tab, click on the down arrow next to credits and select starring
➢ Type in the name of the actors for you movie

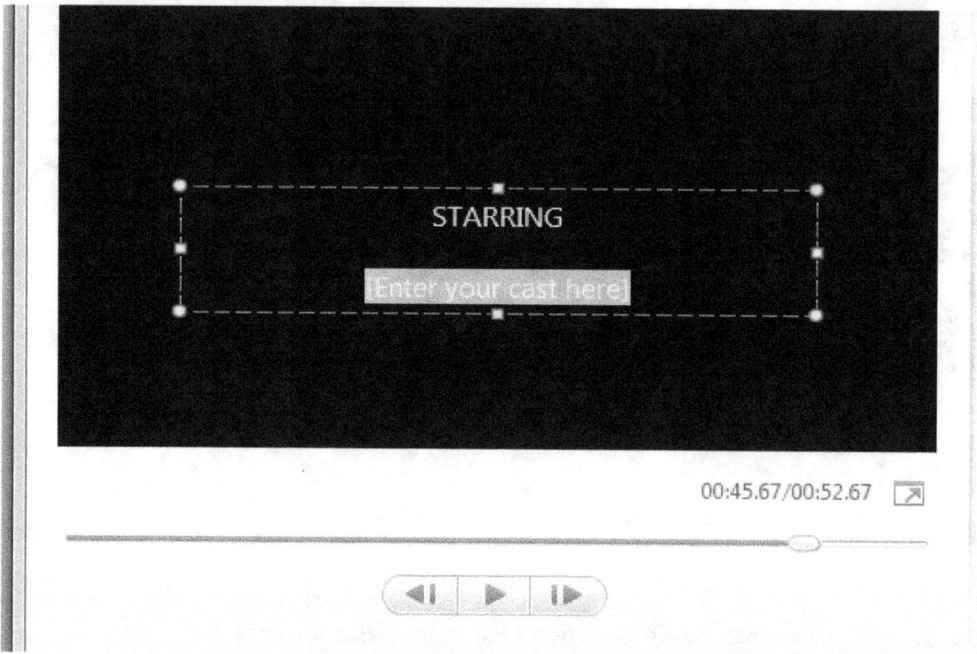

You can move the starring screen to the beginning of the movie by dragging it in front of the other slides

Film location

You can type in where the movie was made

➢ Click on the home tab, click on the down arrow next to credit and select film location

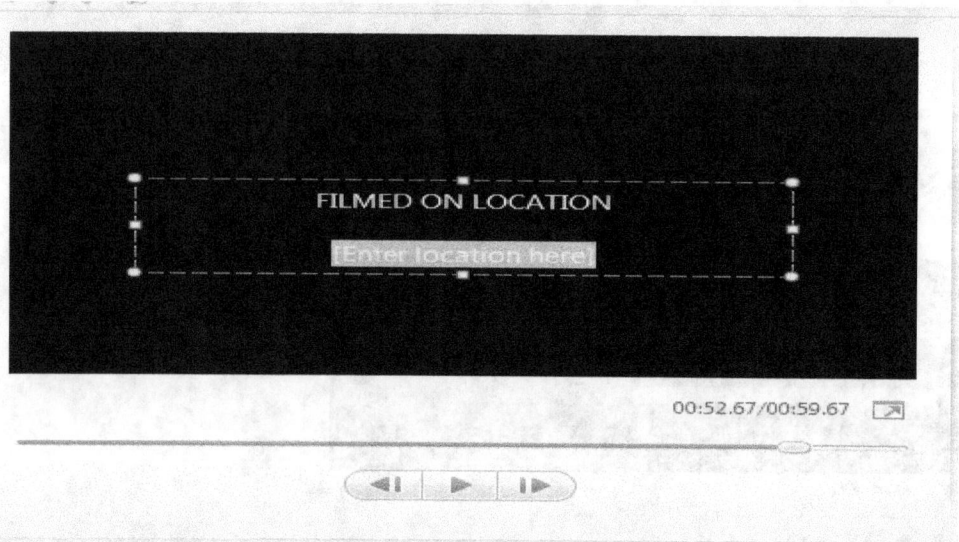

Formatting text

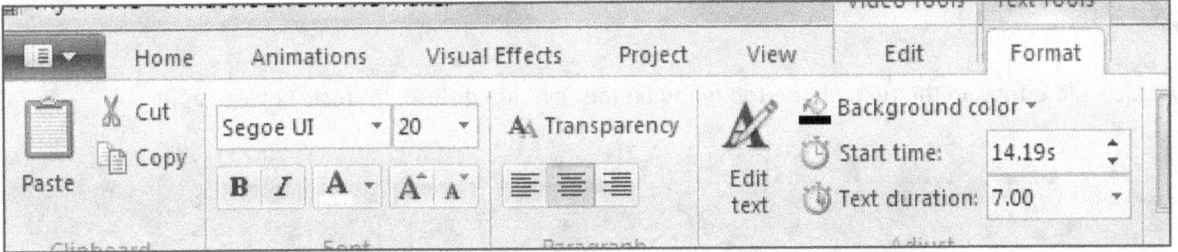

Making the text bigger

- ➢ Click on the down arrow next to the number 20 on the menu on the left side
- ➢ Select 40 to make the text bigger, when you choose a smaller number the text size will decrease

Making the text bold

Click on the B, to make the text bold, the text will appear slightly bigger and darker

Making the text Italic

Click on the I to make the text italic

<u>Making the text underline</u>

<u>Click on the U to underline the words</u>

Choosing a different font style

Next to the number 20 on the left is the word" segoe" this is the current font style, click on that down arrow and choose a different font style

Start time

Click on the arrow to select the start time. The start time is when exactly the text will appear on the screen

Text duration

Click on the arrow next to text duration to specify how long the text will stay on the screen

Effects

You can also add effects to the text, on the top menu on the right are different effects you can apply

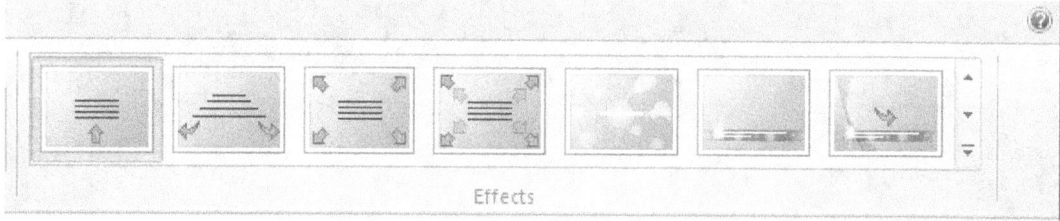

Effect 1 (from left side)

Text will appear from the bottom line for line

Effect 2

The text will swing down

Effect 3

Zoom in small. The text will enlarge slightly

Effect 4

Zoom in big. The text will enlarge slightly

Effect 5
Cinematic burst 1
The text will appear in the center of the screen with a small light and some dots on he screen

Effect 6
A line of text and dots will appear

Effect 7
Dots will appear in the centre and the grey area on the left side will move slightly to the left.

More effects

Click on the down arrow, next to effect 7 will reveal a list of more options

Click on the option of your choice.

The arrow keys indicate the direction that the text will move

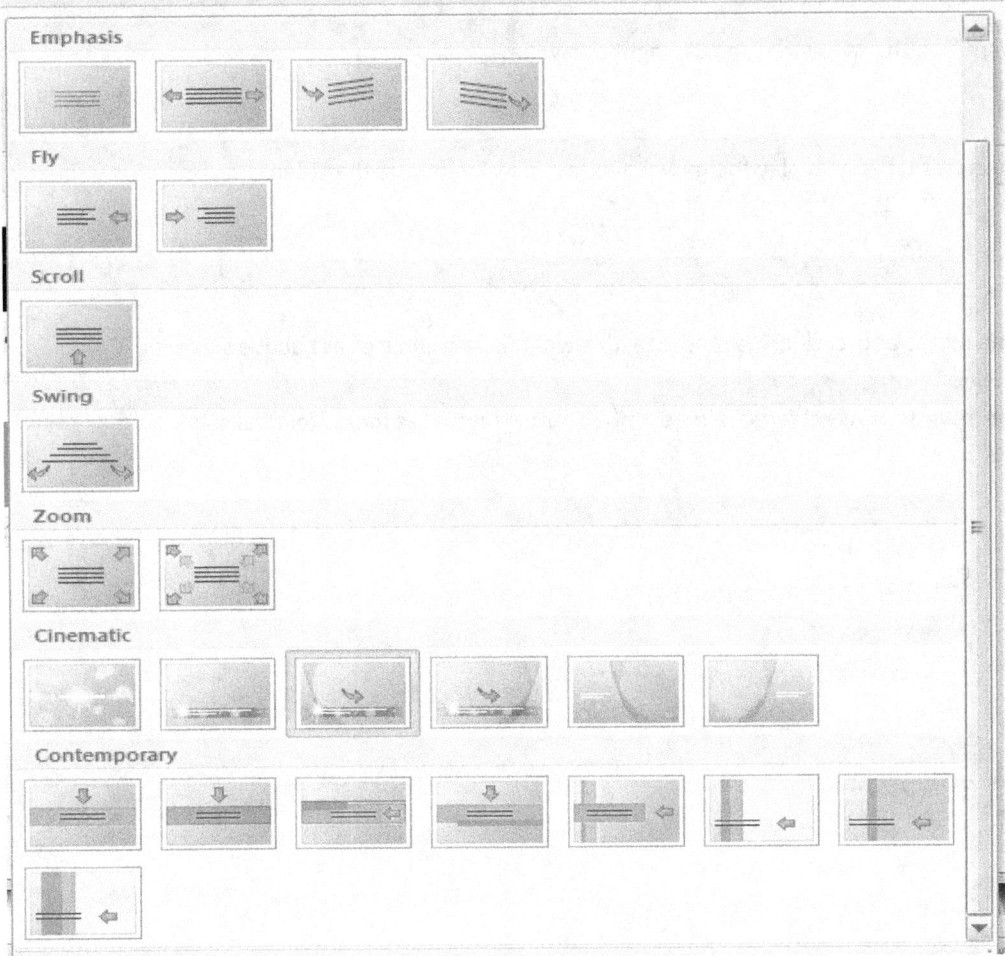

Adding sound

You can add your favourite song to the movie.

> ➢ Click on <add music> and select the music file from the folder where it is stored.
> ➢ You can add a song in the beginning, or play the movie and click on <add at current point> to add music into a certain area in the movie

Thus you will end up with a video that looks very professional.

To play your movie

Click on the right arrow key , the one in the middle

To move back to the beginning of the movie, click on the left arrow key

To move forward into the movie click on the right arrow key

Snapshots

You can take pictures when you play the movie and add it at the end of the video

➢ Play the movie and click on <snapshot>, this will take a picture of the active screen

Saving the movie

You can save the movie to different formats, for example you can save it in a format for a cellphone.

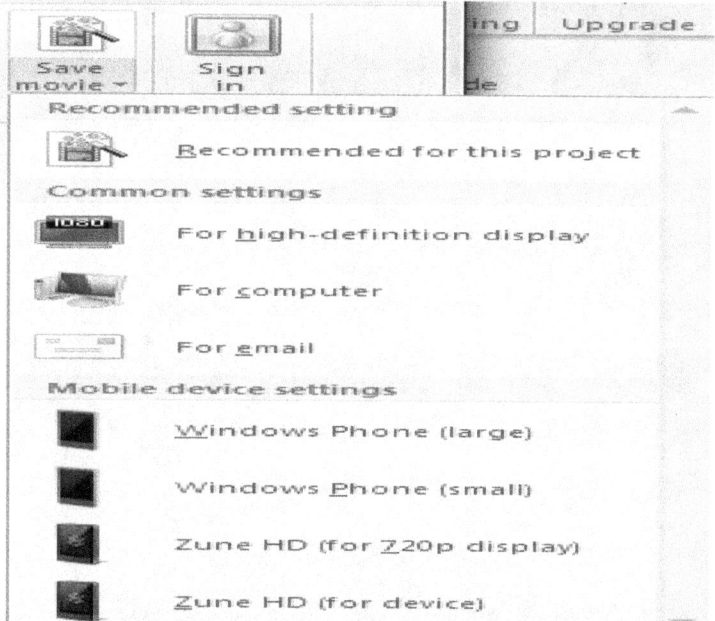

➢ Click on <for computer>to save it for computer

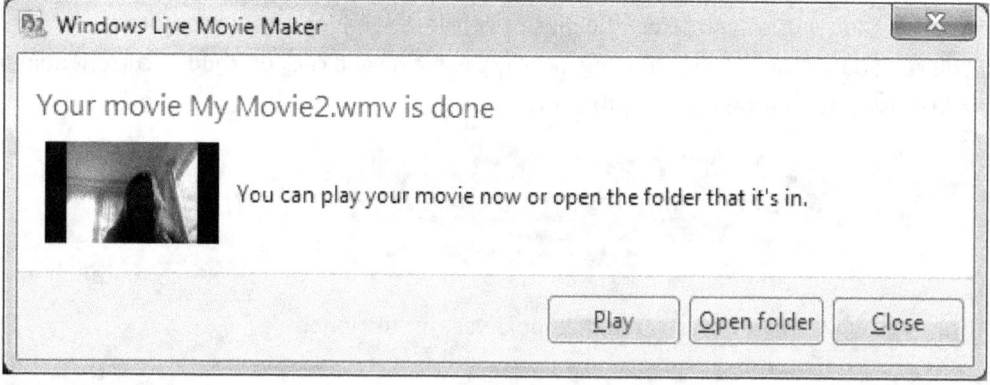

➢

XPS viewer(you can view any document that has an XPS format with the XPS viewer)

Documents can be stored to xps format to protect the data and allow others to read the documents even if they don't have the ms word program. In ms word there is an option to save the file to XPS format

XPS is simply a viewer, to view files that has been saved in xps view and is similar to the pdf viewer

Opening files with XPS viewer

You can open any file that has been saved as a XPS document type.

> Click on File Open

Viewing files in different ways

One page

Clicking on one page will allow you to view the full page on the screen

> Click on the down arrow and select <one page>

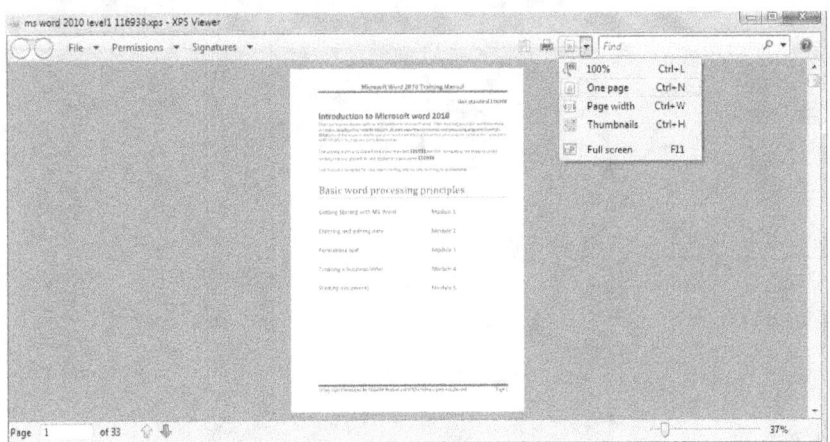

Page width

Clicking on page width will expand the document from the left to the right side of the screen

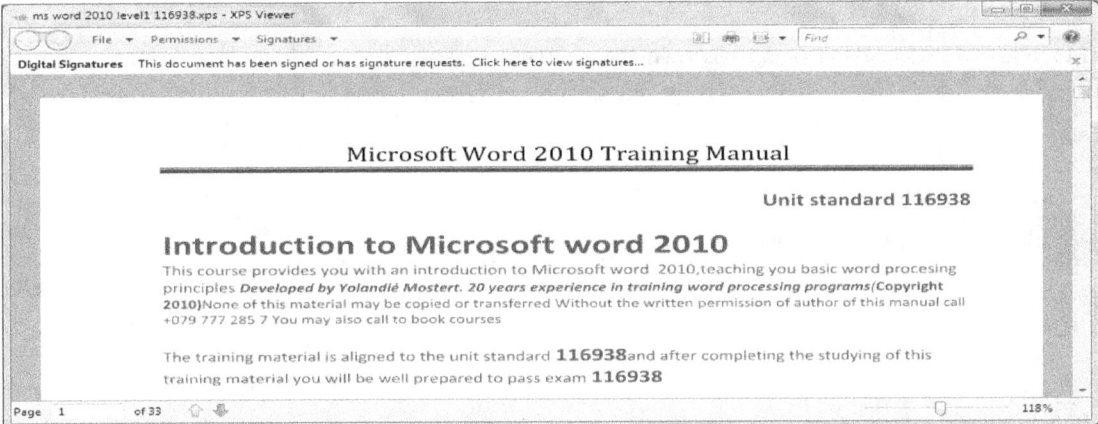

Thumbnail

All the pages are visible on the screen and the page grows bigger when you move the cursor over it.

Click on the down arrow on the menu and select <thumbnail>

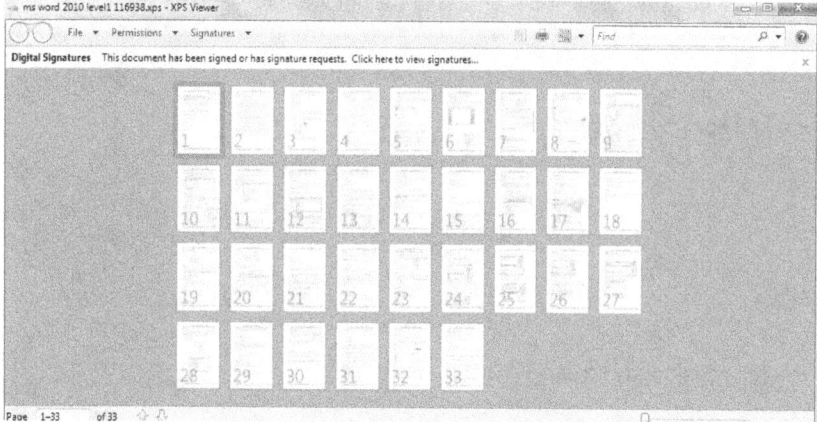

100% view

Click on the down arrow on the menu and select <100%>

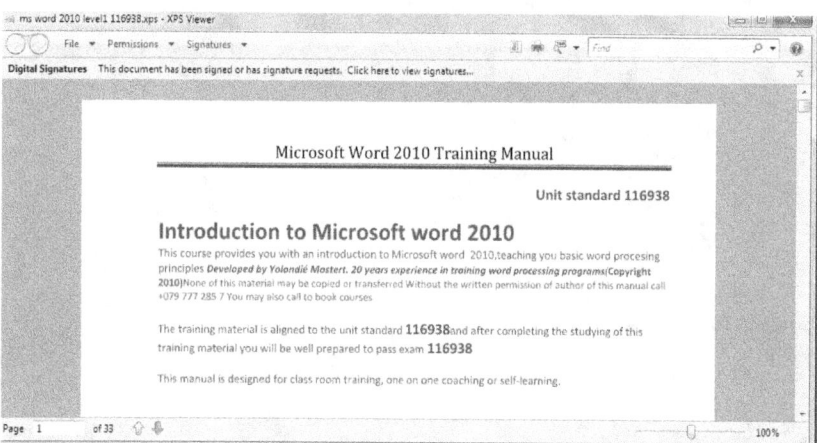

Fullscreen

> ➢ Press F11 to make the document appear fullscreen, the menu will disappear temporarily.
> ➢ Press F11 again or ESC to return to your previous view and have the menu's back!

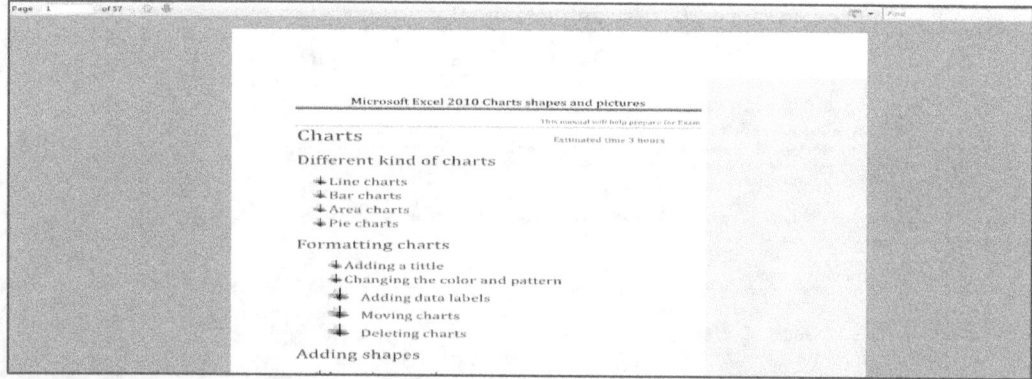

Signatures

You can sign a digital signature on the xps document to validate that this has been your last update and you have made no changes to the document. Thus other documents that doesn't have the digital signature can be shown not to be the final document that you have signed.

> ➢ Click on signatures, sign this document,

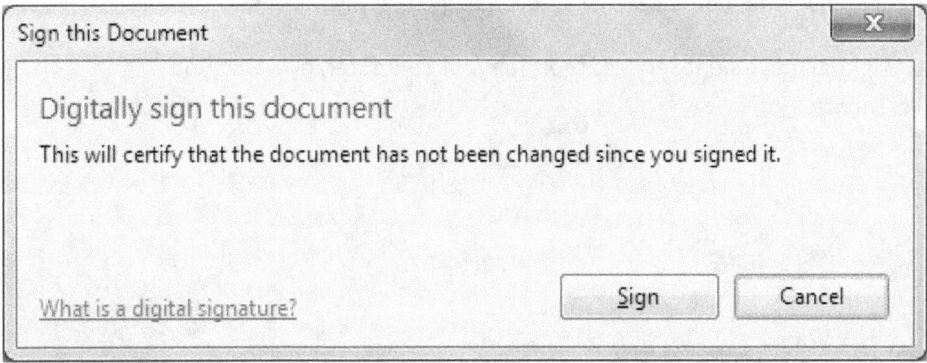

> ➢ Click on sign

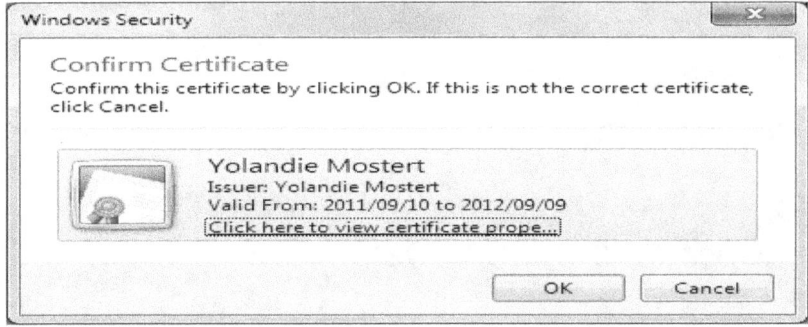

Click to view certificate properties

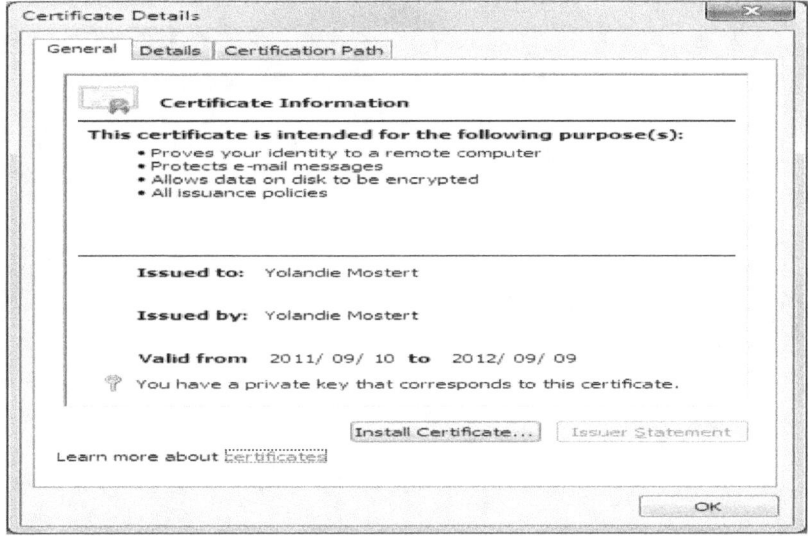

Setting permissions

You can set what type of access users have on the document . You can decide whether a user have read, edit or printing rights, and you can also put a time expiration date on it, meaning the document will only be viewable for a certain period of time.

To set permissions for an XPS document you need to download a windows rights account certificate (RAC)

The xps viewer use windows right management Services (RMS) technology to apply permissions

You can download the windows right management services tools for your computer, however you will have to pay a fee to use this service.

PDF viewer

You can view files that are in pdf format with the pdf viewer

When saving your documents into pdf format, others can read it that don't have ms word and they cannot make changes to your document. In MS Word you can save the document to PDF format

Opening a pdf file

With the pdf viewer you can open any document that has been saved in pdf format

- ➢ Click on file open
- ➢ Select the folder where the file is located and click on open

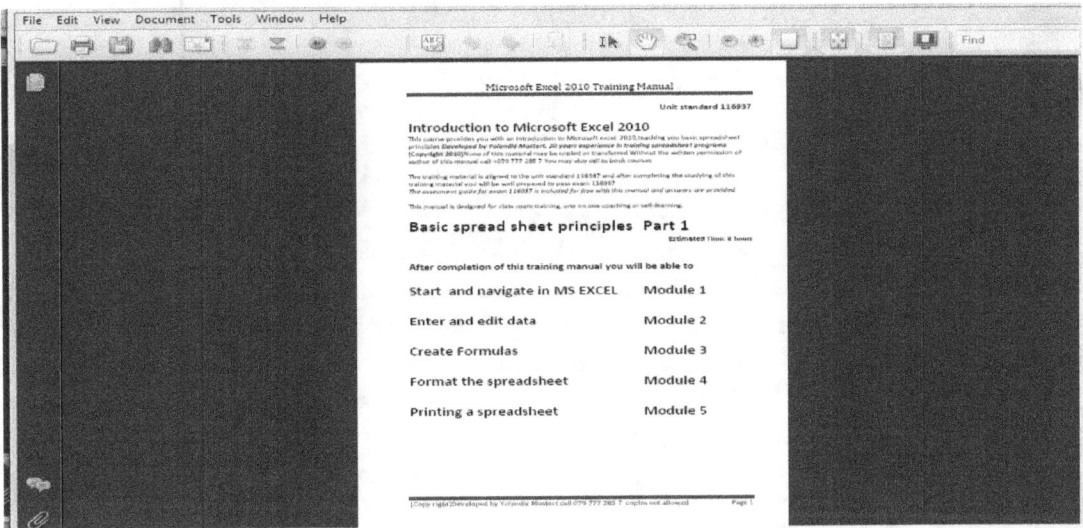

Viewing 2 pages side by side

> Click on page display, two up

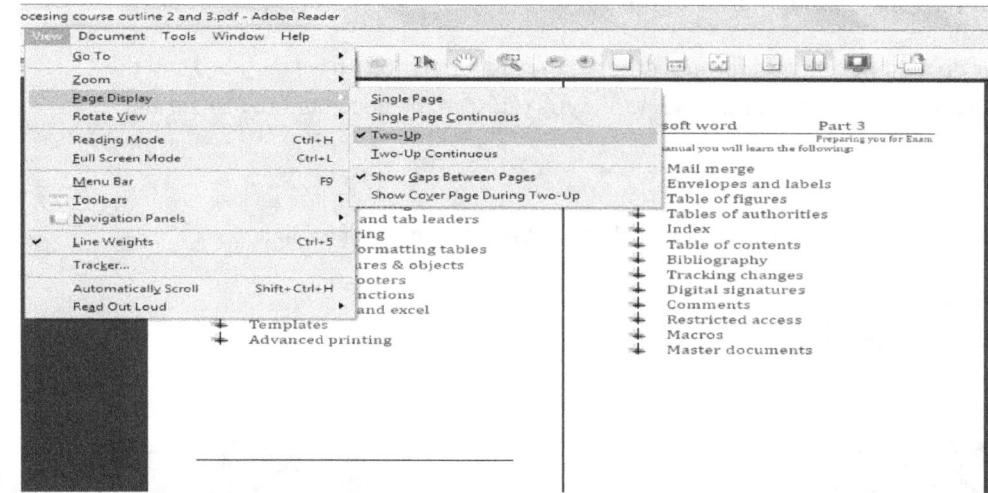

>

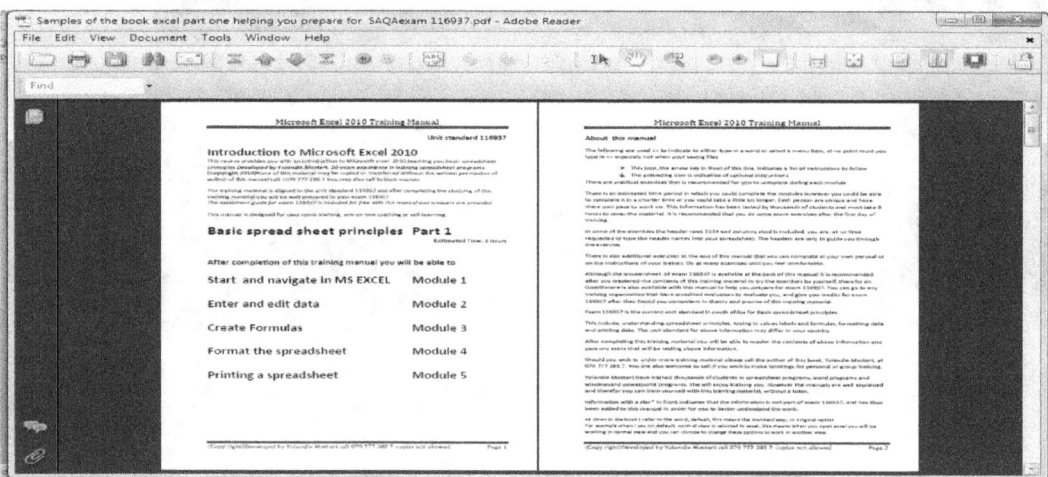

Rotating the page

> **Click on view, rotate view, clock wise**

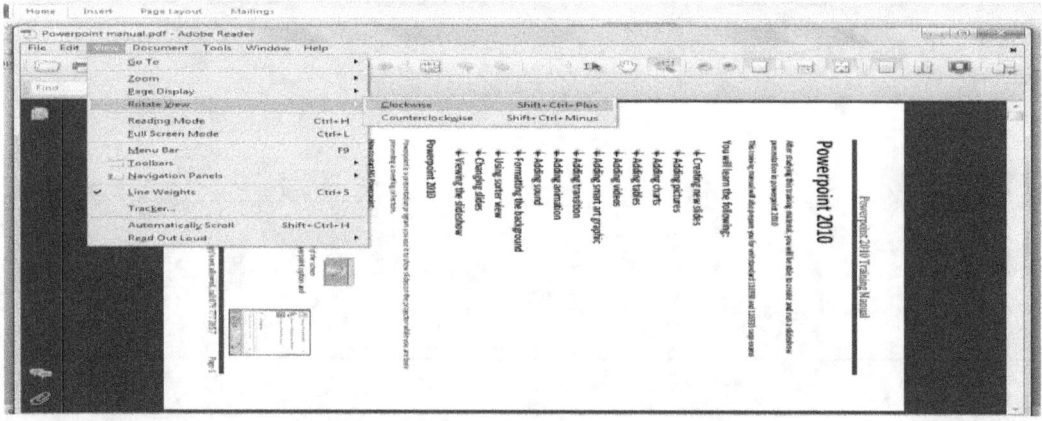

Zooming

➢ Click on the + sign to enlarge the screen a little

➢ Click on the – minus sign to decrease the size a little

➢ Click on the magnifying glass to enlarge the area that you select

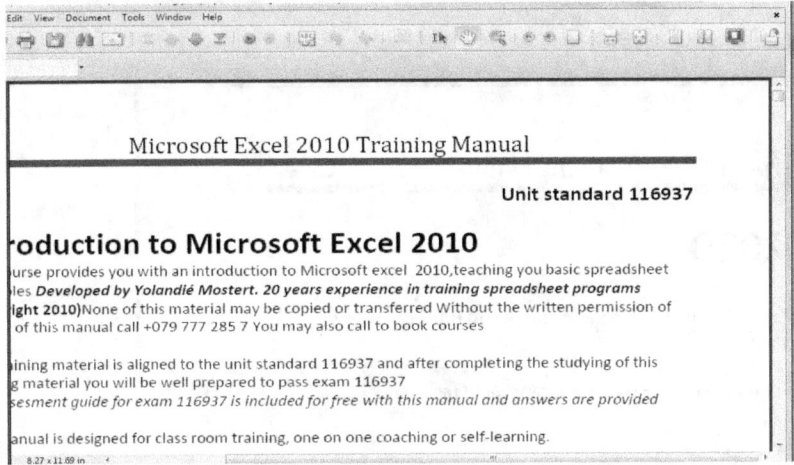

Selecting an area with the magnifying glass

➢ Click on the magnifying glass, and then select the area you want to magnify

2010,teaching you basic spreadsheet
in training spreadsheet programs

Fitting the whole page on the screen

➢ Click on view,zoom, Fit page

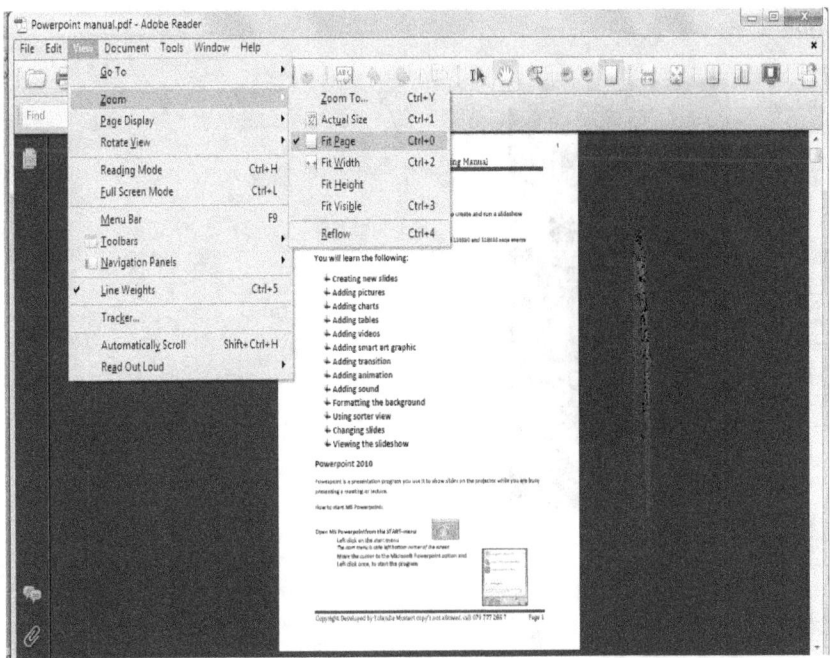

Viewing actual size(100%

> Click on view,zoom, Actual size

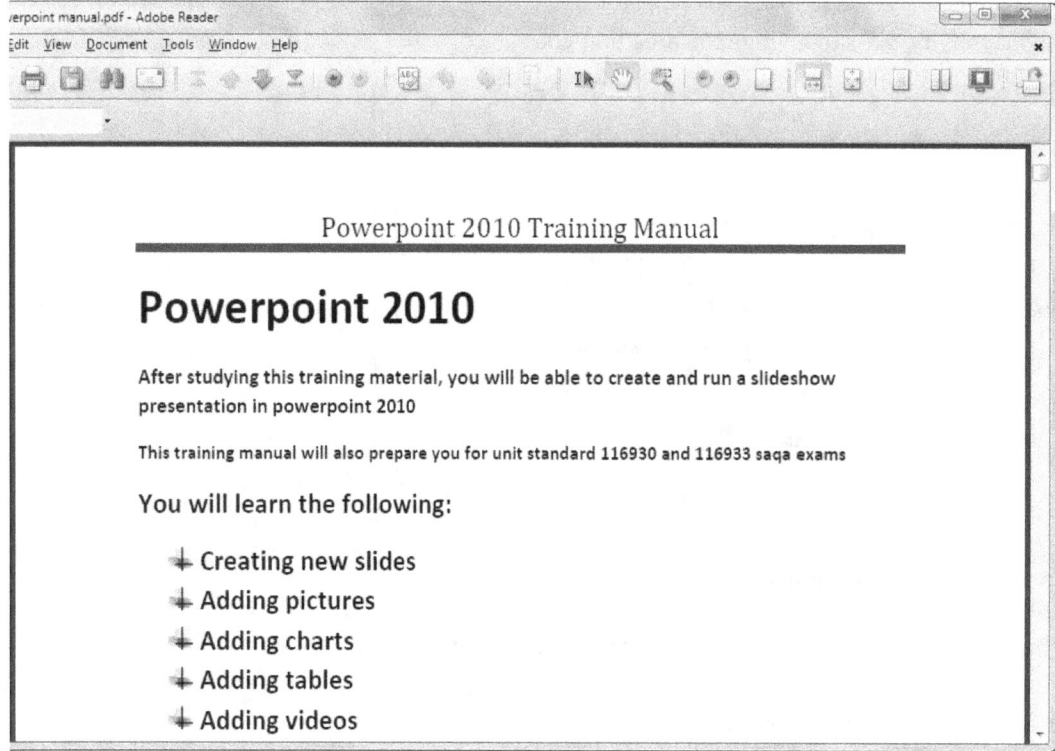

View full screen mode

Fullscreen mode will expand your document on screen and the menu's will disappear temporarily. Press ESC to return to previous view

> Click on view, fullscreen mode

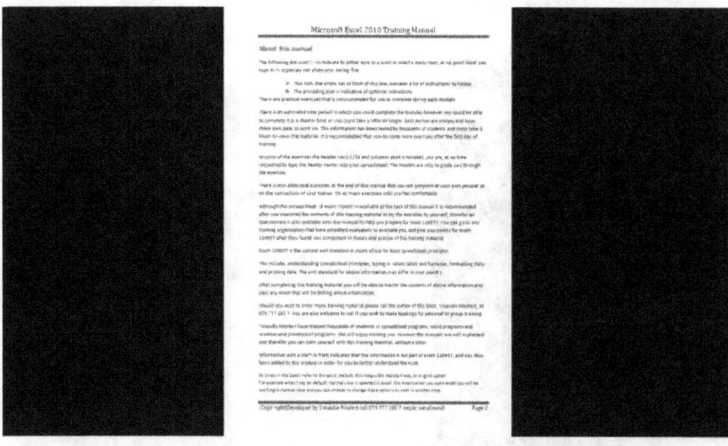

Reading out loud

You can have the program read the document out loud

> ➢ Click on view, read out loud, read to end of document

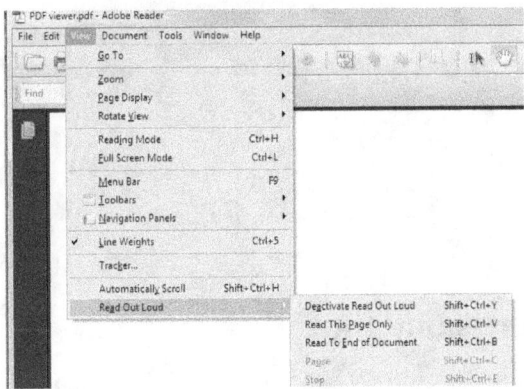

Navigating through the pages

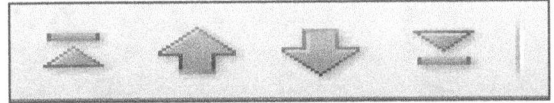

> ➢ Move to last page
>
> ➢ Move to first page
>
> ➢ Previous page
>
> ➢ Next page

Press F4 to use page navigation and then click on the pages on the left side

Press F4 again to cancel this option

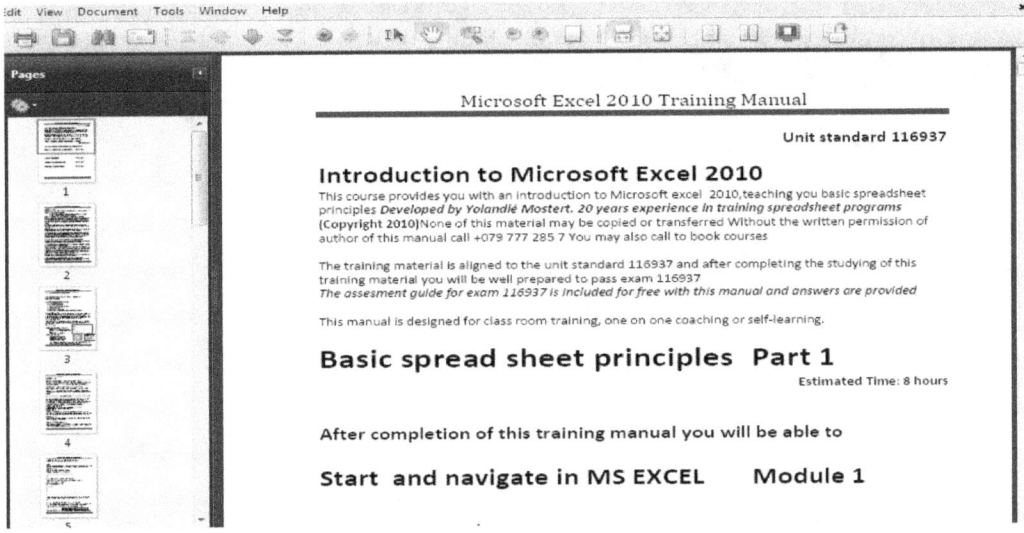

Windows Live Messenger

- Creating an E-mail Account

- Creating new Contacts

- Chatting to a contact

- Chatting to more than one contact at the same time

- Setting favourite's

- Sharing information with contacts

- Using Winks

- Using Nudges

- Saving the chat history

- Setup audio and video devices

- Reconnecting to MSN

- Changing your status

- Changing the default settings

Windows Live Messenger

Windows live messenger , is a special program that you can use when you are connected to the internet, to chat with people, online

In order to use MSN messenger you will need an Email address to log in

Creating an Email account for Windows Live Messenger

In order for you to use messenger you can use a Hotmail account. You will have to go online to create and register an account and you will be requested to provide an Email name and a password for your new account, you will use this id to sign into messenger.

At the messenger login screen, you can click on <sign up> to create your email account for messenger, you need to be online to complete this process

Once you have logged in you will see a screen similar to the one below:

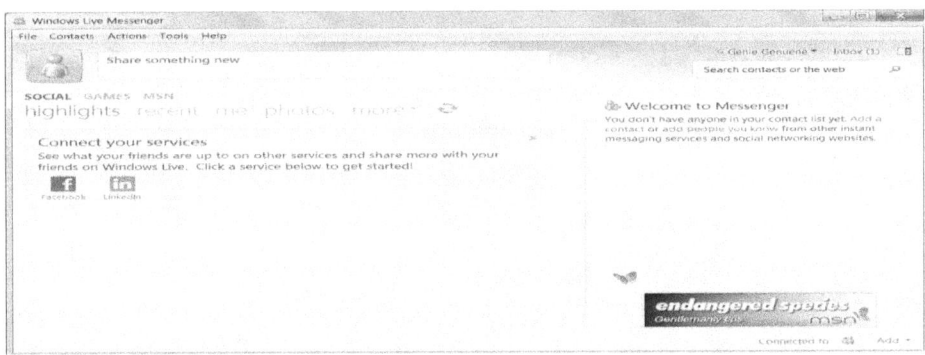

Chatting to your friends

Adding a new contact

To chat to friends using messenger, they will have to supply you with their email address, or they can send you a request that you will have to accept.

To add a new friend to messenger

> ➢ Click on Contacts
> ➢ Click on add contact

Type in the Email address of your friend that you wish to add to your contact list

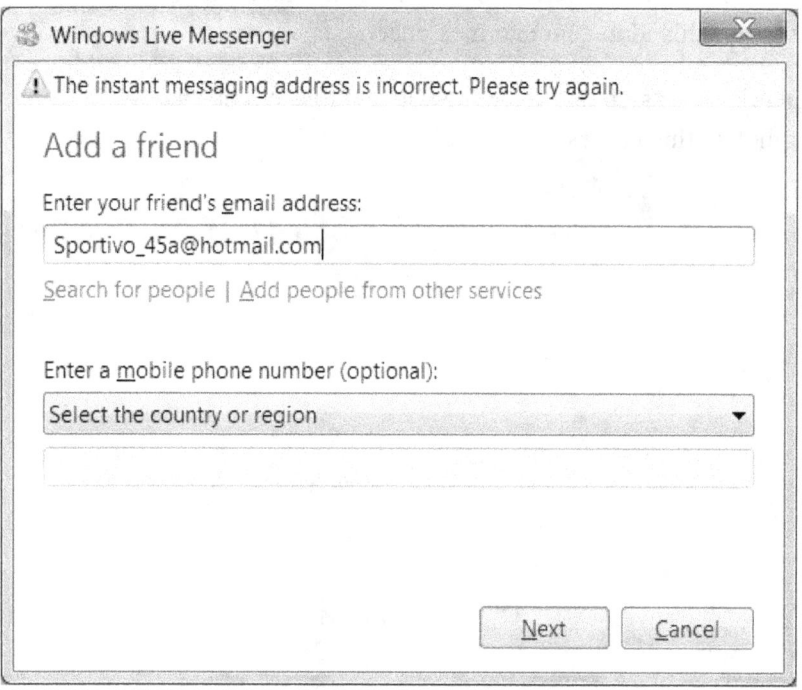

Once you added the email address, click on the <next> button to continue

You do not have to add the phone number; however, you may if you want to

Once you clicked on the next button, the following screen will appear

Favorite

Click inside the square to insert a√ to indicate that you wish to add this person as a favourite in your list. Favourites will always appear at the top of your contacts and you will see more social updates from them.

After activating the favourite option, click on the next button to activate your request, so that you can add your friend to your contact list. The following screen will appear:

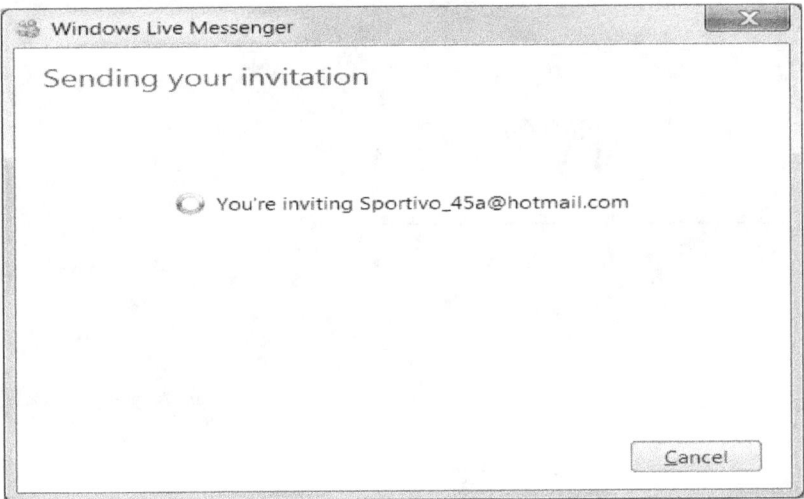

Sharing information with your friends

You can share information with all your friends that are on your contact list.

Type in the information inside the text area at the top left of the screen to share information with all your friends that is on your contact list

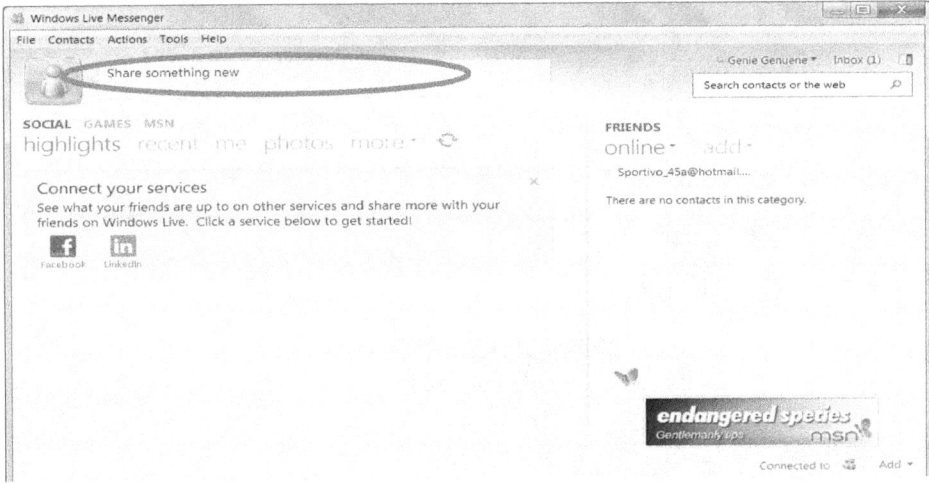

Click on the <share> button to share the information

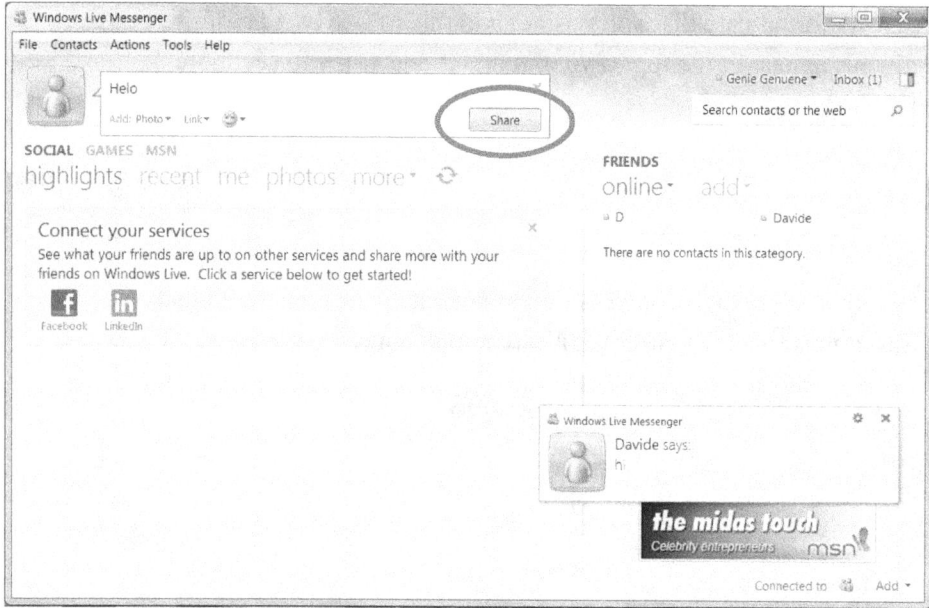

Winks

Winks are animated pictures that will appear on your screen and on your friend's screen that you are chatting to. When you for example click on the wink of the little cat, it will send out a heart, not the purple cat, the purple cat will burb. The wink of the smiley face at the bottom left will start laughing loudly and the wink of the sunflower will make a flower start growing on your screen

> ➢ Click on Actions
> ➢ Click on Winks
> ➢ Click on the wink you want to use

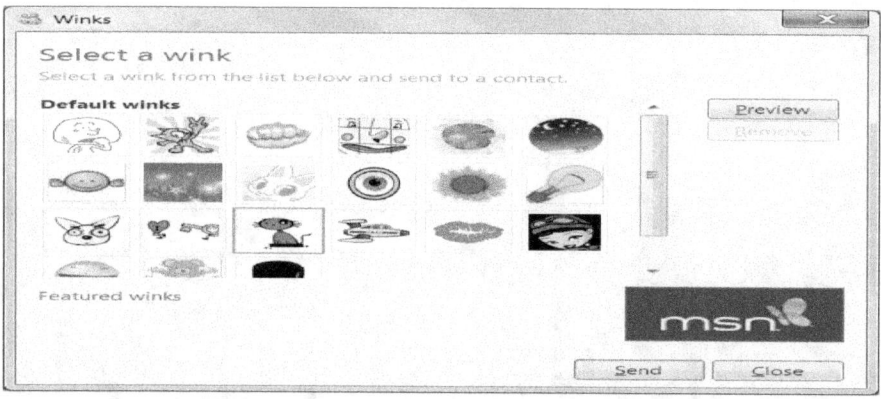

Nudges

When you click on nudge a soft sound will appear on you and your partners screen and it will appear as if the dialog box is shaking, you can use a nudge to get the attention of your partner online when you are trying to chat to them and they perhaps are surfing the net

- ➢ Click on Actions
- ➢ Click on Nudges

Conversation with your partner

When you are busy, chatting this is what the screen will look like

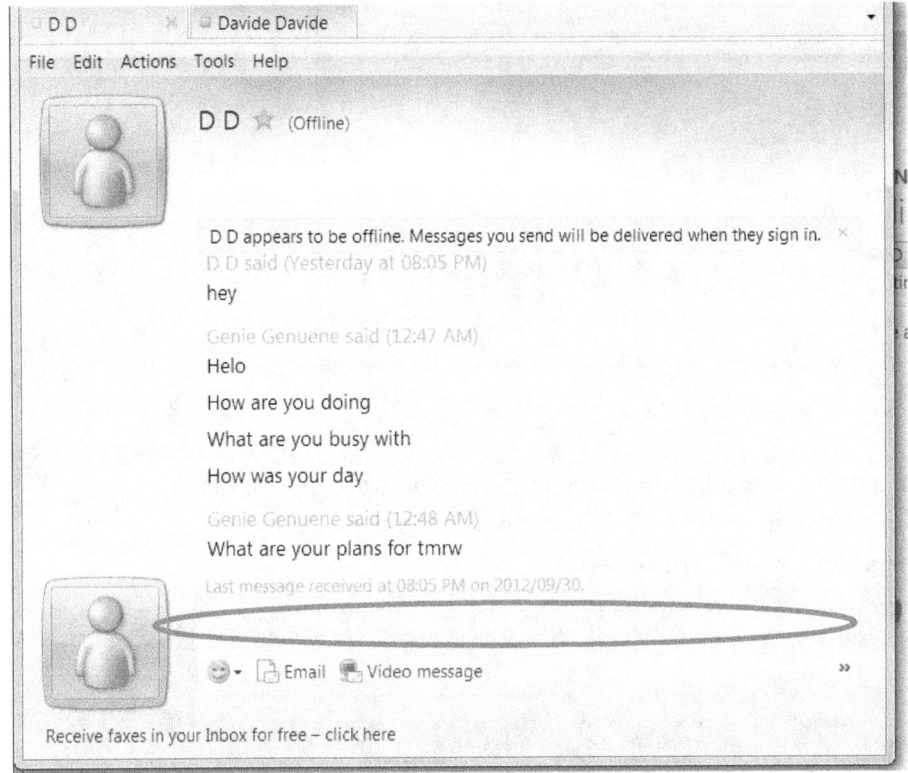

The new information that you wish to type in, are typed in at the bottom of the screen, and your friend's information appears at the top of the screen.

You can also send an Email, a video message, or a special icon by clicking on the smiley face, if your friend is not online, they will receive all the messages you typed when they go online.

- ➢ Simply type in the information you want and then press the <enter> key for the message to be send to you friend

Chatting to a friend on your contact list

A list of all your contacts will appear at the top right of your screen

Simply double click on the name of the contact that you wish to start a conversation with and a dialog box will open where you can chat with that friend in private without others on your contact list being able to read your information

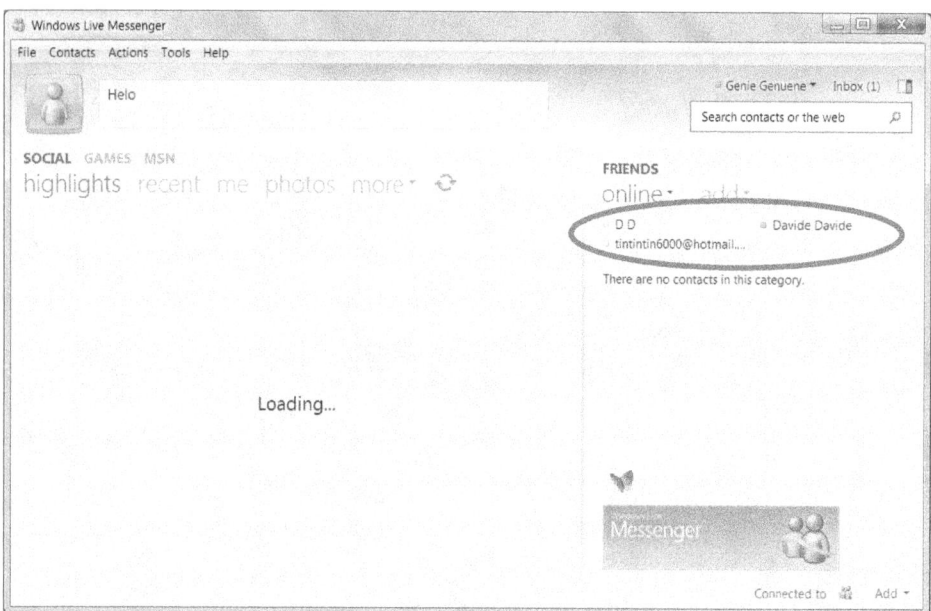

Saving the Chat history

When you choose to quit msn, a dialog box will appear requesting if you want to save the chat history, when you click inside the little round circle and a blue dot appear next to the yes option it means that the conversation you had will be saved.

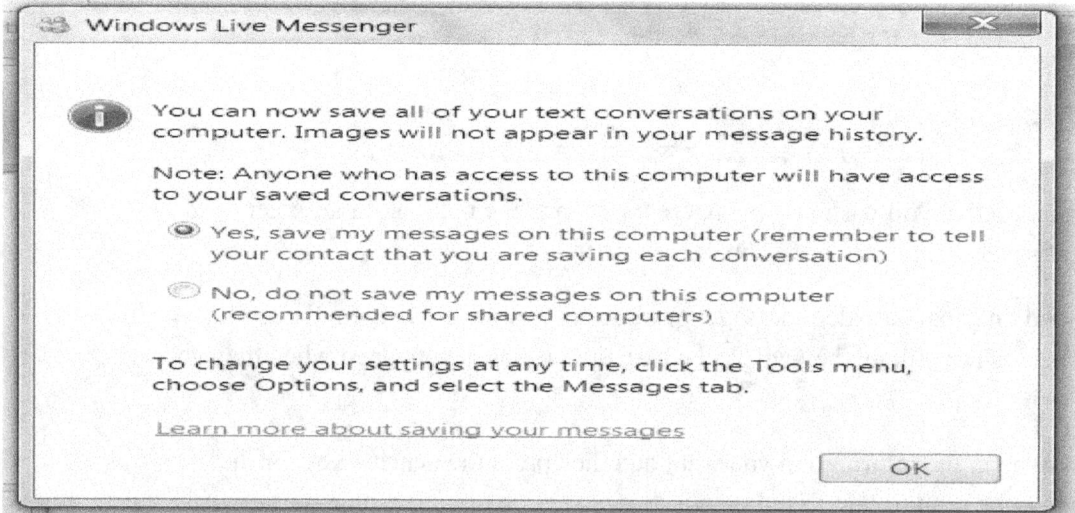

Chatting to more than one contact

You can chat to more than one contact at the same time

> ➤ Click on <invite a contact to join this conversation

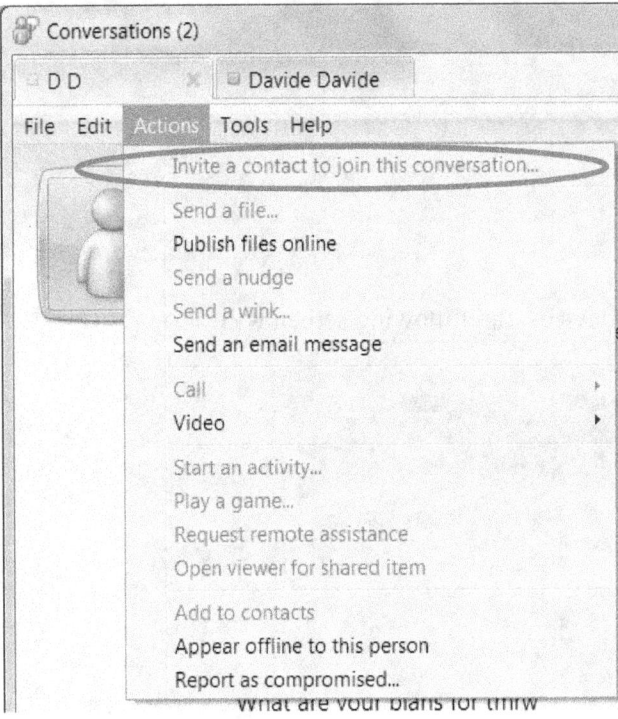

View chat history

If you have saved your chat history, you can simply click on the <view conversation history> link to view the previous chat session.

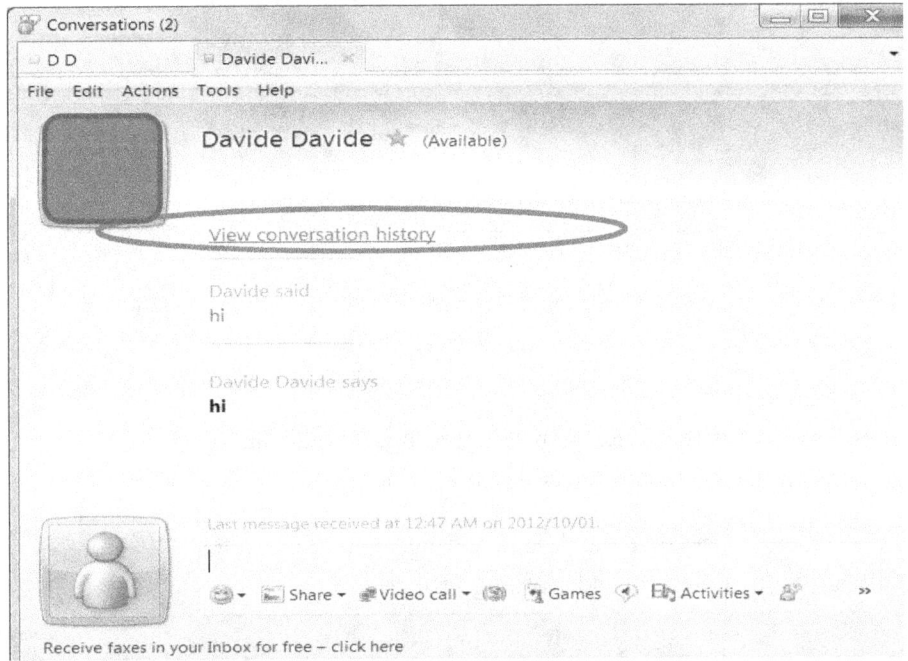

Set up audio and video devices

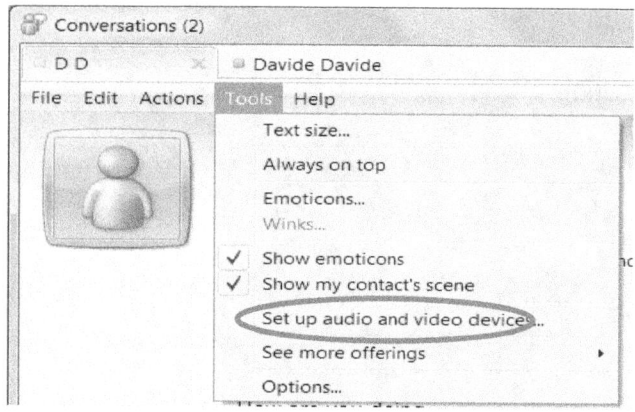

When you click on the option, setup audio and video devices ,the following screen will

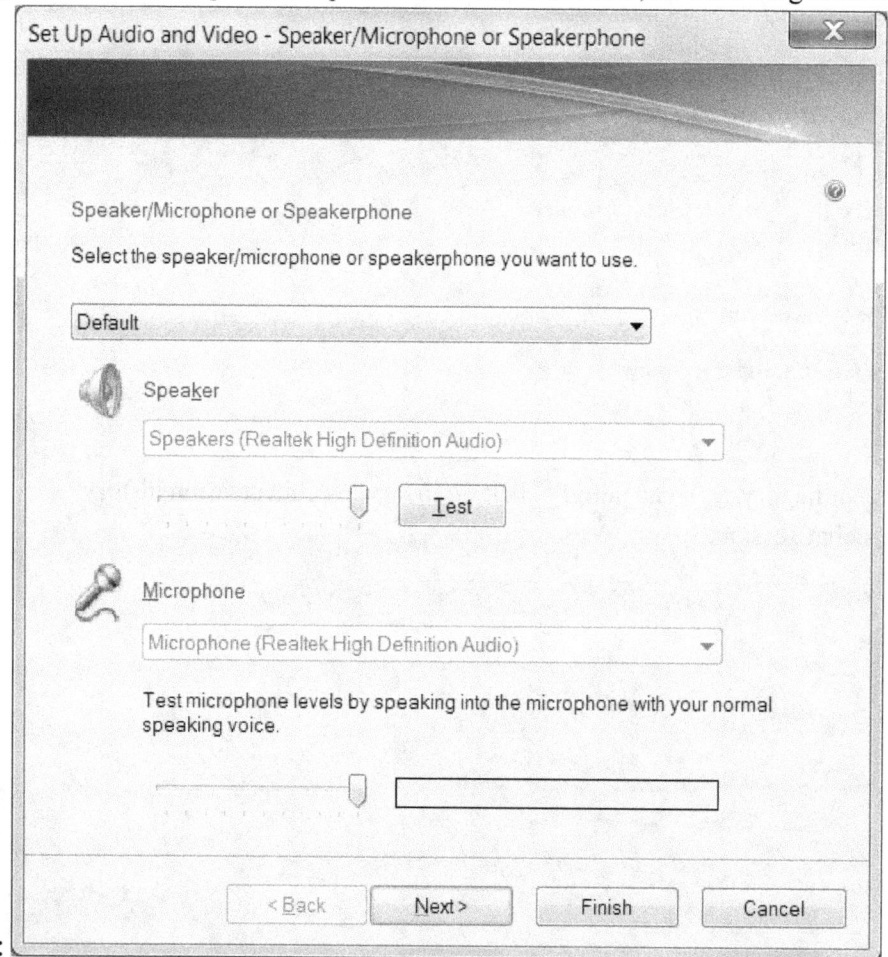

appear:

Change the settings to your desire and then click on test, to test the sound, if you hear some music when you click on the test option, then it means the sound is working.

If you are not sure what settings to change, just leave the default settings, and click on test, chances are that your audio is already setup correctly and working properly

Once you tested the microphone, click on the next button

The following screen will appear

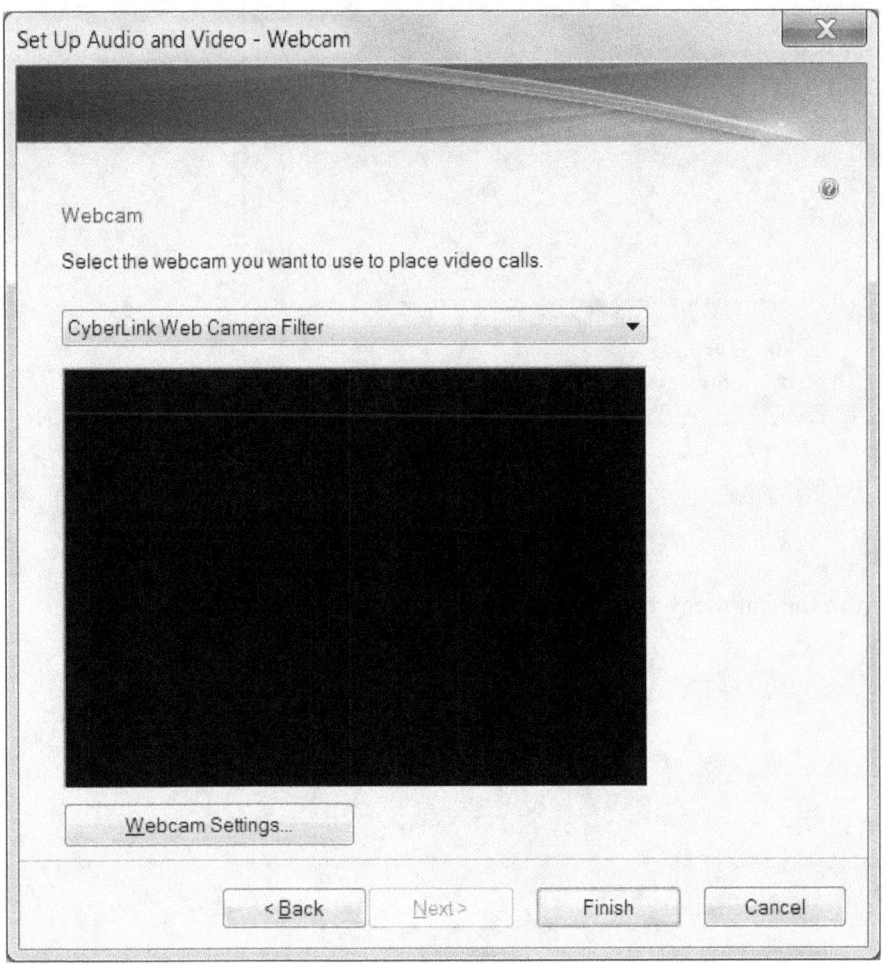

Testing the webcam

Messenger can also allow you to voice chat with video, therefor it is important to make sure that your web cam is set up correctly, if you can see yourself on the screen it means that your webcam is working fine and you can complete the process by clicking on the finish button.

If there is just a black screen, like the example above and there is no picture of you on the screen then it means that you will most probably need to change the settings in order for your web cam to work,

> ➢ Click on Webcam settings, to setup the correct settings for the web cam

Click on Advance

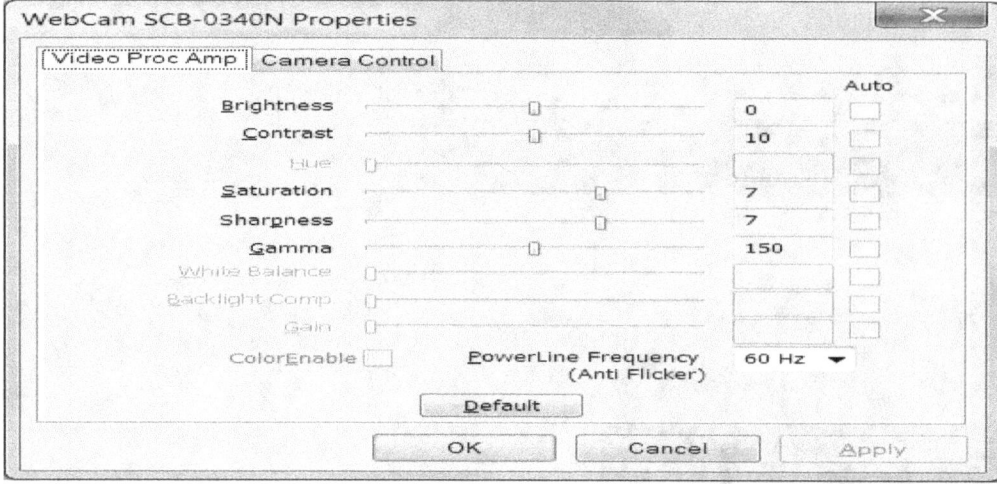

Reconnecting to MSN

If you have been disconnected from the internet, you will find a button on the right bottom of the screen to re-connect to MSN

> ➢ Click on connect

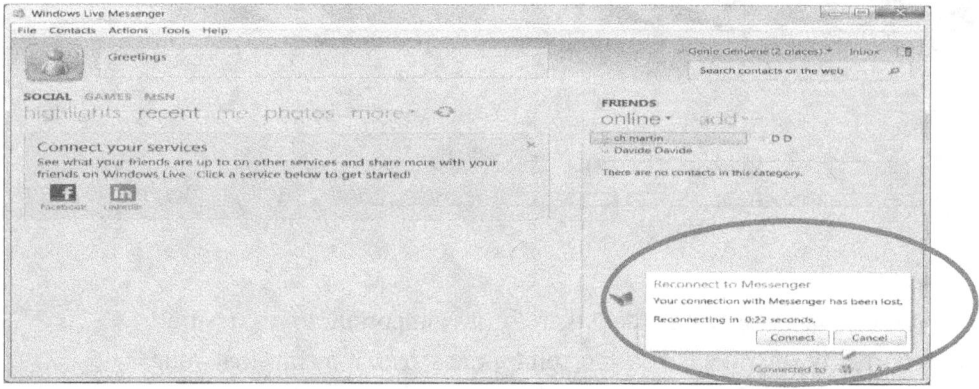

Changing your status on MSN

When you sign into Windows live messenger, your friends will be able to see that you are online; however, you can change your display to any of the following options

You can select to be <busy> so that your friends do not bother you or you can

Select to be <away> so that your friends can know that you are busy making coffee and not at your computer at the moment, or you can select o be

Offline so that no one will know that you are online and you can work without anyone bothering you

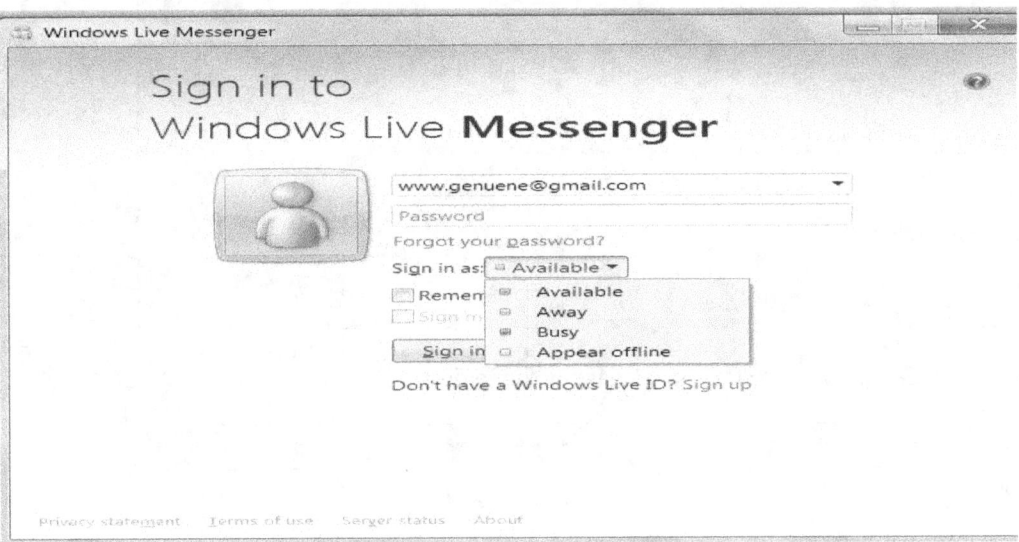

When you are busy logging in, your screen will appear as follows:

You can change the following settings

To change your settings, click on the <options> at the login screen

The following screen will appear, allowing you to make changes to the default settings

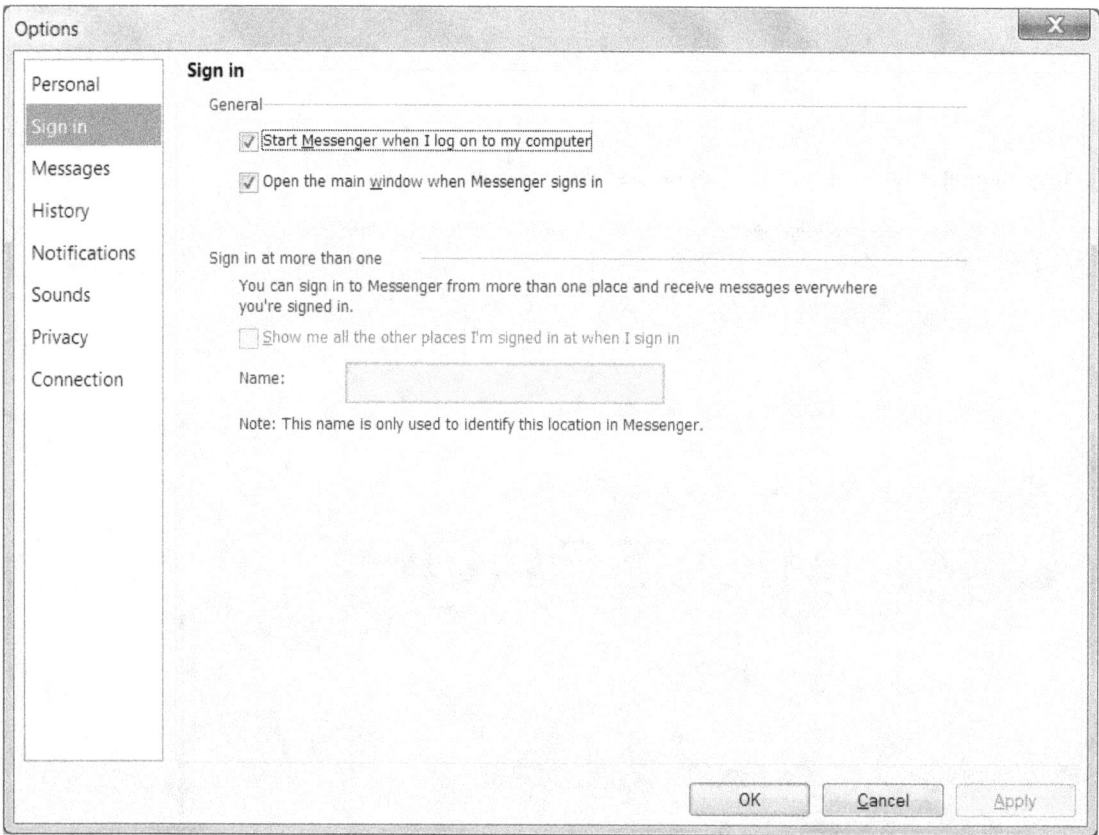

Messages

You can select to show emoticons and timestamps on messages and automatically accept voice clips, nudges and winks

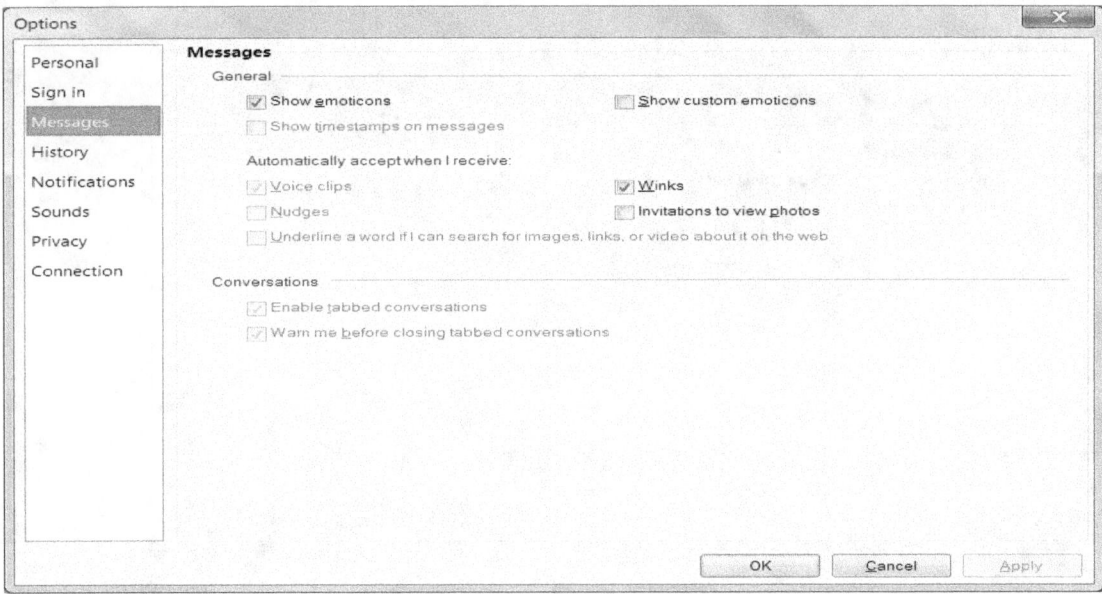

History

Your history files are automatically stored on the default file location; however, you can change this by clicking on the change option

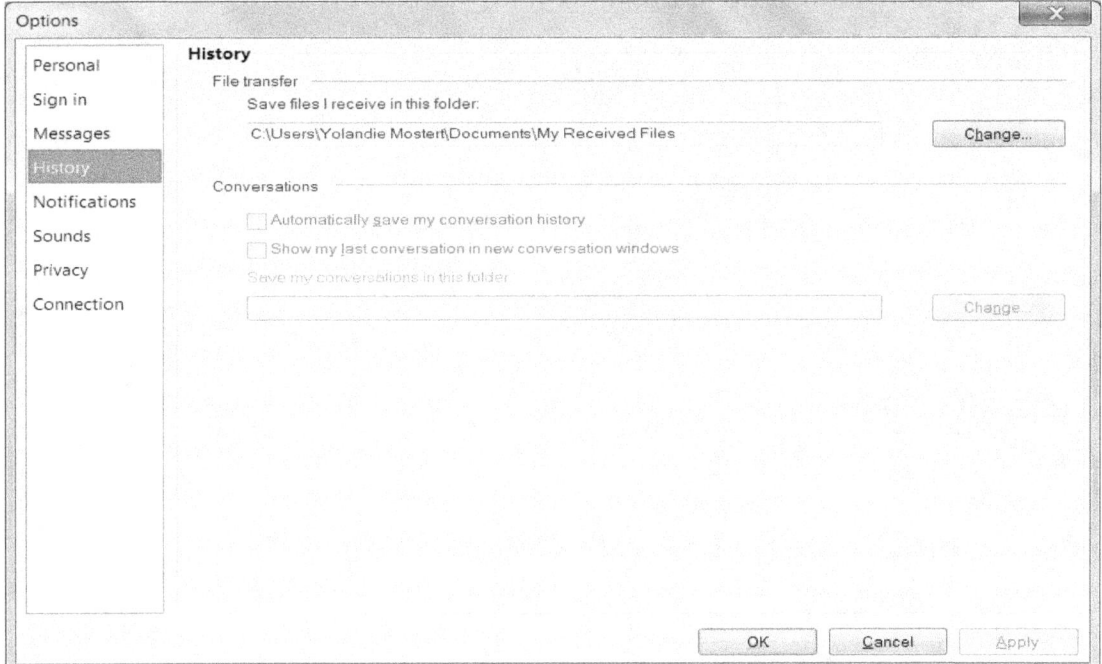

Notifications

You can select to have MSN notify you when a favourite or a friend have signed in and when you have received an IM or EMAIL

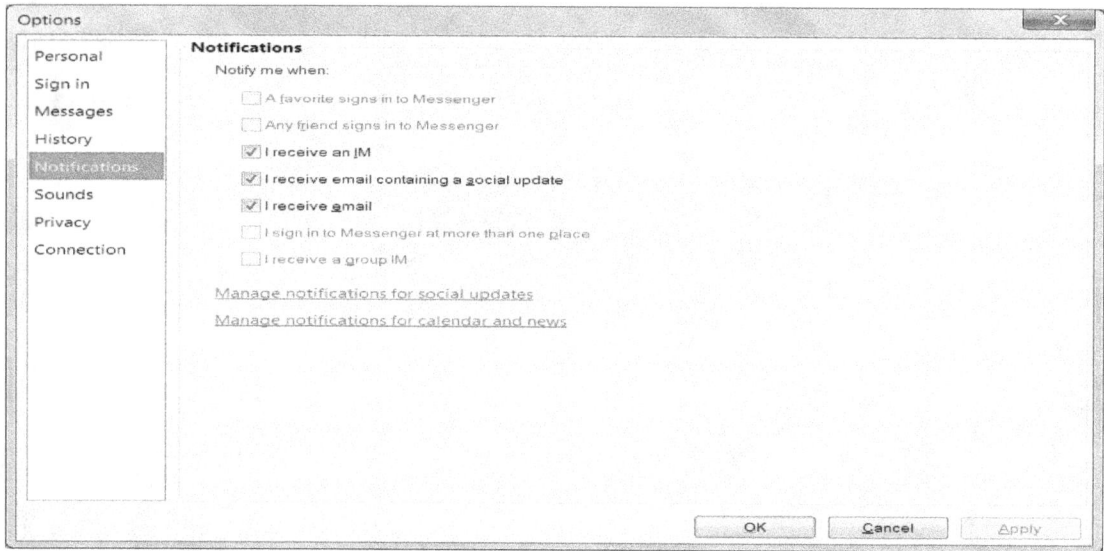

Sounds

You can select to disable sounds by selecting the mute all sounds option

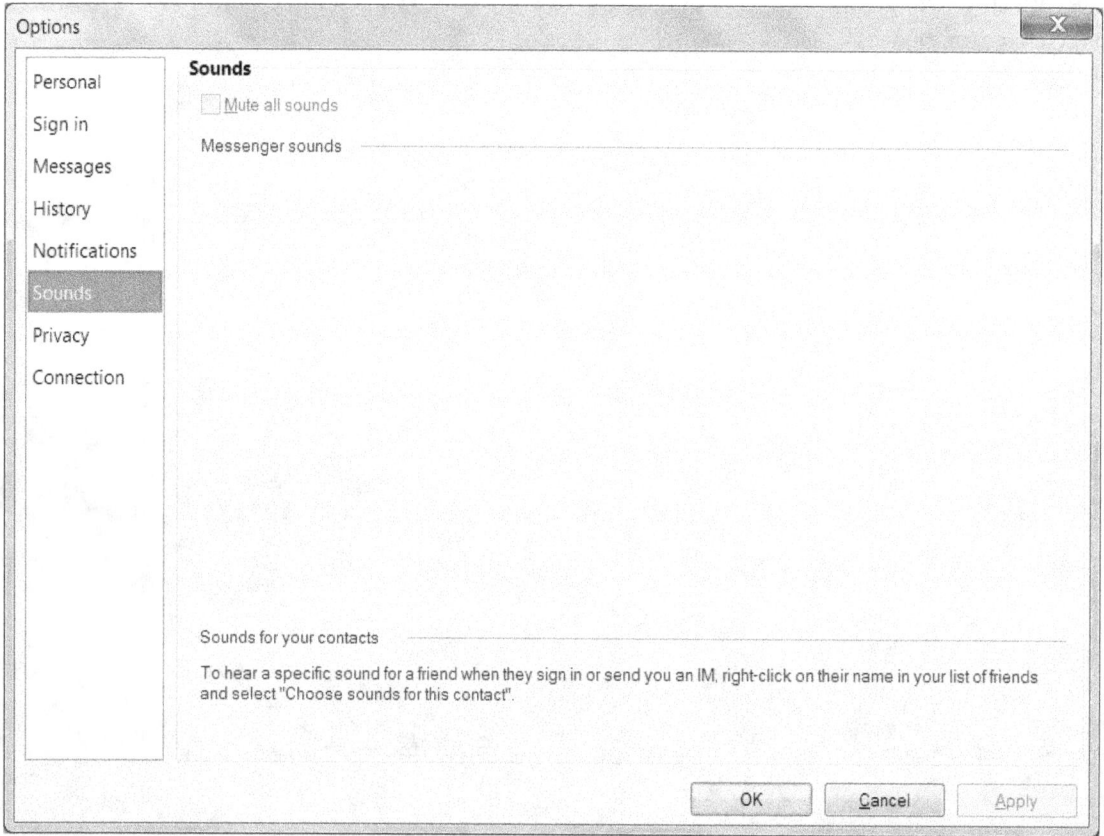

Privacy

You can select, not to have your contact list and social updates stored on the computer

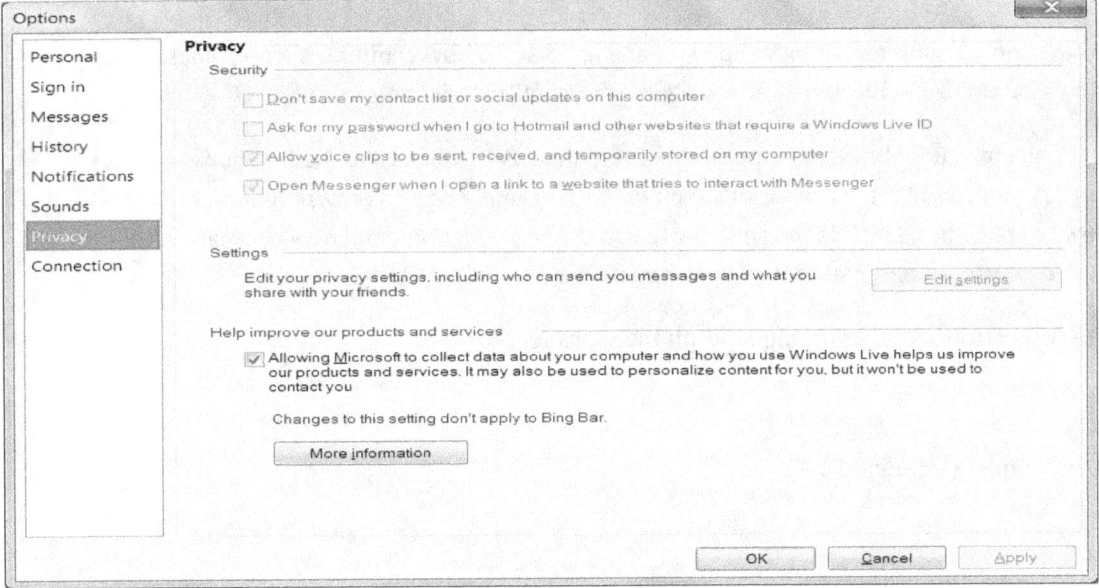

Connections

You can select to save a log of your server connections to help troubleshoot connection problems

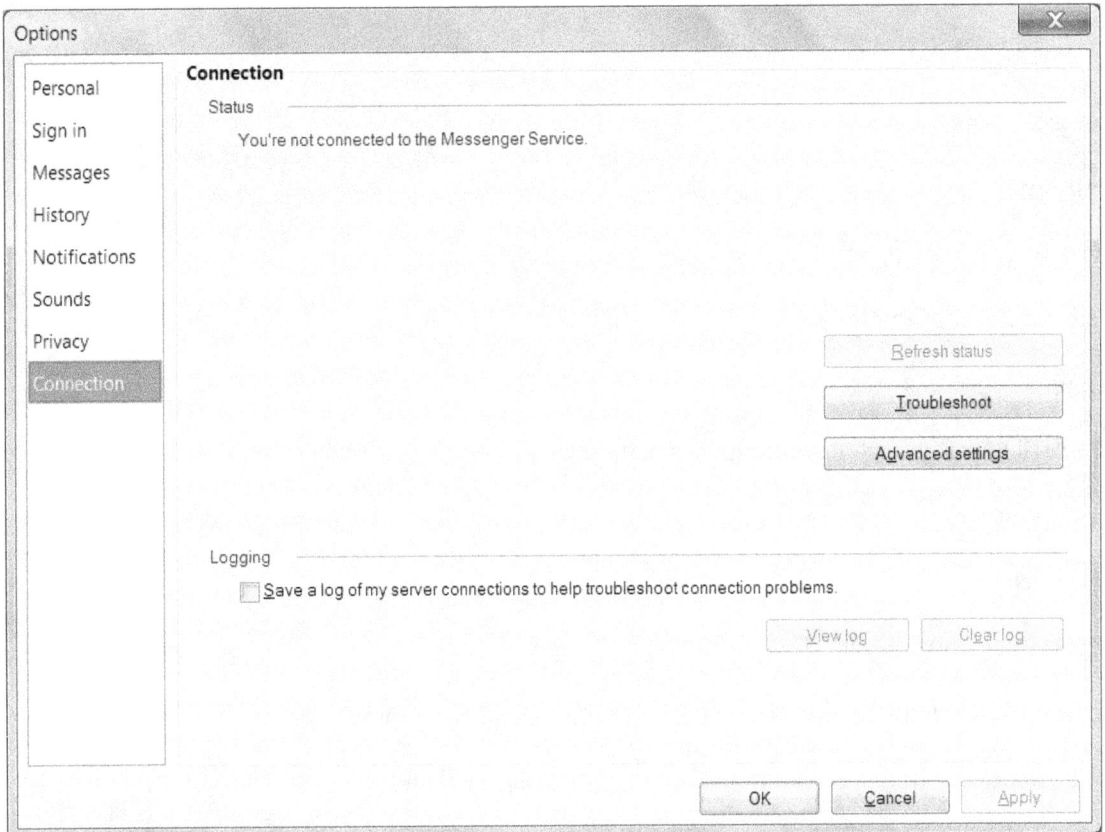

You have reached the end of this book, however there are many more books that you can read, please go here:

If you wish to have more details regarding Windows 7 and understand how computers work, please buy the **Windows 7 training manual part 1** at www.lulu.com/spotlight/worldpeace734

The Windows 7 training material exist of 2 books, this one Windows 7 Utilities and the first book Windows7 part 1, that have all the functions of windows 7, for example how to browse files and folders and how to create files and folders, and how to use the help functions, and how to create user accounts and how to set parental control on windows 7

The following Microsoft books are being sold on the website

Windows 7

Microsoft 2010 Training manuals

Word,Level 1,2,3

Excel Level 1,2,3

Powerpoint

Outlook

Access

Html Web programming

Soft skill training

How to be an effective team member, Team leader

Managing and supervising Employees

How to be Happy

How to find a perfect partner and have a happy marriage

How to quit smoking

Creating World Peace

How to get everything you want in life

How to educate children How to discipline Children without spanking them

You can go hereto order: http://www.lulu.com/spotlight/worldpeace734

By helping to distribute these books you will not only be making good money, you will be helping in implementing world peace. By educating people we can create less conflict in the world and move a step closer towards world peace.

This book's designed by Yolandie Mostert copyright©2014

You will need written permission to make copies of this book

You can contact Quality1Training@gmail.com

You can order digital copies in PDF format here: QualityTraining.Yolasite.com